Awareness:

Creating your own balance in life

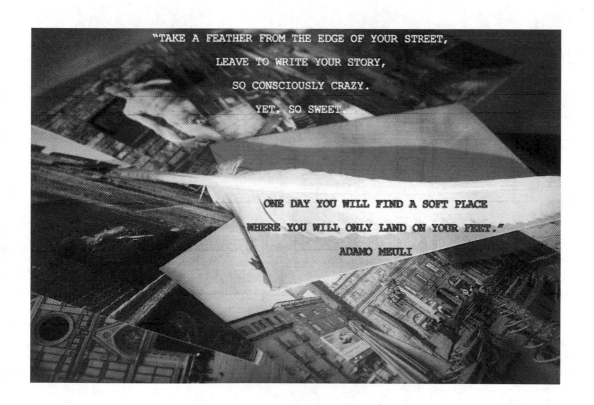

"TAKE A FEATHER FROM THE EDGE OF YOUR STREET,
LEAVE TO WRITE YOUR STORY,
SO CONSCIOUSLY CRAZY.
YET, SO SWEET.

ONE DAY YOU WILL FIND A SOFT PLACE
WHERE YOU WILL ONLY LAND ON YOUR FEET."
ADAMO MEULI

WWW.AWARENESSINLIFE.COM

Balboa Press books may be ordered through booksellers or by contacting:

Balboa Press
A Division of Hay House
1663 Liberty Drive
Bloomington, IN 47403
www.balboapress.com
1-(877) 407-4847

Because of the dynamic nature of the Internet, any web addresses or links contained in this book may have changed since publication and may no longer be valid. The views expressed in this work are solely those of the author and do not necessarily reflect the views of the publisher, and the publisher hereby disclaims any responsibility for them.

The author of this book does not dispense medical advice or prescribe the use of any technique as a form of treatment for physical, emotional, or medical problems without the advice of a physician, either directly or indirectly. The intent of the author is only to offer information of a general nature to help you in your quest for emotional and spiritual well-being. In the event you use any of the information in this book for yourself, which is your constitutional right, the author and the publisher assume no responsibility for your actions.

Any people depicted in stock imagery provided by Thinkstock are models, and such images are being used for illustrative purposes only.
Certain stock imagery © Thinkstock.

Printed in the United States of America

ISBN: 978-1-4525-4972-9 (sc)
ISBN: 978-1-4525-4971-2 (e)

Library of Congress Control Number: 2012906822

Balboa Press rev. date: 6/7/2012

WHY CREATE AWARENESS?

Natasha Rocca Devine:

'Awareness' to me is like having a sixth sense. It is the ability to understand life on a deeper level and to live present in each moment. On one level, it is seeing and appreciating beauty in the simplest of things. Yet, it equally embraces the complexity of people and all challenging things in life. Most importantly, it embraces a freedom of the past, aiming, but not living in the future and embracing the concept of living now.

'Awareness' enables us to see life beyond our own lenses, which frees us from the idea or concept of living 'in a box'. Instead allows us to move into a place of creativity, balance, acceptance and authority in each moment. Of course, always having time to laugh. Humour is essential to happiness.

For myself, the most significant change on my path of 'Awareness' occurred after a serious car accident at 19 years old: when I was in a coma, after suffering a Subarachnoid hemorrhage and injuries to my jaw. I was extremely fortunate to have American surgeons who saved my life and prevented me from brain damage and remaining in a wheelchair. Evidently, it was a life-changing experience, which in an immediate sense, left me extremely ill due to the accident, tablets etc. Later on, my co-ordination was off balance so I found walking and daily activities very difficult. At a time when my peers were advancing, I had to retrain myself in these simple actions. Along with significant memory loss, I was overwhelmed and off balance.

At this time, I was advised by surgeons and physicians worldwide that I must take various tablets each day for years to follow, that I would not continue my studies in college, work may be too much pressure and there was no option to travel and live a 'normal' life. Prior to the accident, I was extremely health conscious, exercised daily and was very active in each day. So, I will not deny it was a tough recovery to undertake with each day being a challenge both physically and mentally. Yet, I refused to accept this life set out for me. I knew that I was strong enough to overcome this alone and without tablets. So, I cut all medication and began my journey of 'Awareness'.

As I was determined to return to my health as before, I tried many self-healing and alternative practices to find solutions. At times, I have and often push myself too hard and end up worse off. So, I now know balance and living in the moment is the answer. In this book you will see many ways that I have tried and tested such as Acupuncture, Bikram Yoga, Energy healing and other options that had been recommended by friends, family and colleagues. Some helped me on a physical level and for a day or so I felt better. Yet, it was a time when although I wanted immediate solutions, I looked for a long-term solution(s) to keep myself in balance.

Thankfully at this time, my mum shared the practice of 'Metamorphosis' with me. After a few months training with Ireland's top practitioner, Margaret Boland, I saw fundamental changes in my health and balance. Unlike other practices Metamorphosis does not just treat the symptom but moves directly to the cause of the block. Through treatments, the clients and the practitioner shift blocks, which allow you both to live in the moment and in balance. What I like mostly about this practice is that it is self-healing without dependency, control or force. The practitioner is merely a catalyst for change. The responsibility is on each individual. Since then, I have trained as a practitioner in order to share this practice with clients, family and friends. Aiming each day, to share, live and practice a life in balance for both myself and all that I meet on my path.

Months and years after, my recovery defied all the surgeons' predications. So, I now know that balance begins within. Plus, I see my accident as merely a moment in time that opened up my idea of Awareness. It is in the past. Yet, from this moment, I now know that you can create anything you wish for in life. I am shocked when hearing of a quick-fix route to happiness. Worst of all, people who are trying living a life of 'perfection'. It is an abstract concept with no relevance to you or I and adds unnecessary pressure on everyone. Happiness=balance in each day.

What is definite is that, if you find your own balance and inner strength then you can overcome any block or fear in life. This will then allow you to live and enjoy each day and create the right solutions in the moment. I still insist that being in balance must be a daily commitment to yourself. One must focus on the positives and realize your significance in the bigger picture. In life chaos creates only chaos, as does strength permeate strength, light shines through light and 'Awareness' of yourself creates inner strength and allows others freedom to do so.

Now, as a writer, lighting (and through this book graphics) designer, my sensitivity is in my essence and adds to my 'Awareness'. For work, communication of my ideas, is part of my skillset. Along with my healing, there are other areas of life that enhance my 'Awareness'. Such as, traveling to over seventy cities, studying and working in my beautiful home of Dublin along with the cities of Boston, London, Milan, Los Angeles, San Francisco and Vancouver have assisted this process. Along with each person I have met to date.

Alongside these, others that have constructed my path of 'Awareness' are my friends, family and my parents specifically. My dad, who is a coach and former professional footballer for Ireland, Arsenal F.C. and various other teams, reminded me of the importance of health. He insisted in achieving the balance between reaching your goals, whilst enjoying each day.

"SPORT CONNECTS US ALL IN ONE SPECIAL MOMENT." NRD

My mother, a former Television Broadcaster and writer, shared with me the power of Communication and Self-Healing through Metamorphosis. My sisters, brother, niece and all of the Rocca and Devine family members, individually and collectively, share with me the concept of love, laughter and living life in balance.

Ultimately, my story is my own. Yet, this is about embracing yours and you. Creating this book took me many attempts, all of which added to my Awareness. It reminded me that we can create anything we wish for in life, in the moment and in balance. Most importantly, when focusing on our own truth, overcoming obstacles and having faith:

"Don't tell me that I won't, I will
 Don't tell me how to think, I feel
 Don't tell me 'cause I know what's real
 What I can do." Joss Stone

Through my interviews, I aim to shed light on the concept of 'Awareness' of others. In the remainder of the book, I wish to share these options through my writing, typography and graphics. With this insight, I hope you will find your own balance, creativity and light.

With 'Awareness' I wish for you to enhance your quality of life, even more than you had imagined possible:

SO THE POWER OF EACH MOMENT
WILL COME TO LIFE.
AS WILL YOU.
AS YOU DESERVE."

"Viva Per Ora."
NATASHA ROCCA DEVINE

WHAT DOES **AWARENESS** MEAN TO YOU?

Christine Adamson, Mother and Fashion, Theatre and Media Make Up Artist, Ireland:

"Awareness for me is living life in a conscious state, a present state, I think the most important purpose in our lives is to be present, if we are lucky enough to have had a glimpse of awareness, which I have, then I can make a conscious choice to be present in everything I do. Once awareness happens to you, you cannot reverse it, you are awakened, but it can be delayed by the ego.

Awareness for me also means to live without ego and in this 21st fame-crazed century that we live in, that is hard! But we do have the responsibility nonetheless to recognise awareness as the most important thing that can happen to us in our lifetime, if we are one of the lucky ones, we can then live our life with quality, care and attention in absolutely every single thing that we do."

Reggie Bostic-Alleyne, Executive Events Producer, Boston:
http://www.reggiebproductions.com/

"Awareness is keeping your wits about you in a world where anything can happen. Dreams are made and just as easily destroyed by the simple lies of jealousy. If we continue to believe that goodness still exists in the world, we just might have a fighting chance to expose these lies and live out our dreams."

Javier Garcia-Alzorriz Barrenengoa, Interior-architect, London and Spain:

"Awareness is the perception that we have of each situation and the way that we have of thinking, analysing and facing situations. Awareness is that little voice inside our mind, which guides our feelings, emotions and actions.

Each experience in life changes our awareness. I believe that one of the meanings of our life is developing an honest and strong conscious in order to become a better person, be happy and make the people around us happier too. I think that our awareness can be trained to develop a better us."

Amy, Actress, Dublin:

"I see Awareness through people and their Awareness of themselves and of others. A little mindfulness can go along way.

I recently lost a friend to depression. Having heard this devastating news in the early hours of a Friday morning, I found myself wandering around town. I had nowhere to go but also didn't really want to be on my own. I was simply, walking. After an hour or so of aimless meandering, I came across a cafe and decided I needed to stop for a tea. Perhaps my emotional state showed on my face, but as soon as I entered this busy cafe I was greeted by the most wonderful waitress I'm certain I will ever meet. She had the most beautiful, warm face. She oozed Loveliness.

I didn't have to say a word to this woman. She could see that I was upset and she knew she was going to be incredibly kind to me. She showed me to a corner table, away from the main bustle of the cafe but not too isolated. She talked me through the menu, smiling widely as she did.

I ordered and she came back two minutes later with my tea and a huge slice of cake, which I hadn't ordered and wasn't charged for.

I left soon after and even thought she was now serving someone else, she made a point of saying goodbye to me. I'm sure this woman is as kind and lovely with all of her customers. I just hope that she knows how much her kindness meant to me on that difficult Friday morning."

Katherine Barrett, Student and Athlete, Northeastern University, Boston:
http://spinachandspandex.wordpress.com/

"To me, awareness means recognizing the connection between your mind, body, and the world around you. It is easy to get caught up in one of the three, but without recognizing the importance of the connection, you can never truly be aware of each and every moment, action, or thought. Awareness is essential to life. Without it, you can never truly experience anything."

Sophie Bicknell, Interior Designer and artist, London:

"Awareness is not being afraid to open yourself up to the world around you, having the hunger to question what the world shows and the strength to find your light amongst it all. It is seeking out knowledge from the darkness, however difficult and never hiding from what you find."

Ad Bradley, Music Director, Ad Bradley Music, London:
www.adbradleymusic.co.uk

"Awareness to me is to keep a perspective of the bigger picture always, not get caught up with the moment - try and keep a balance whether a drama or an ecstatic period (being conscious of the affects of both physical and mental), easier said than done, however it's my mechanism."

Margaret Boland, Metamorphosis practitioner and coach to Natasha: http://www.metamorphosis-rstjohn.com/

"Awareness is the manifestation of consciousness. Thought is the manifestation. With the practice of Metamorphosis we have more access to consciousness as we release blocks. With increased awareness we can take positive action to live a creative life."

David Broderick, Director, Broderick's Snacks Ireland: http://www.brodericksbrothers.com/

"To me, Awareness is nothing without the ability to act on it. For example if you are crossing a road and are about to be hit by a bus- Being 'aware' of it is not going to be much use to you!!"

Lou Buglioli, Chairman and CEO of Viewpointe, New York: http://www.viewpointe.com/

"A willingness to listen, to understand and to challenge oneself and others."

Elaine Buckholtz, Light Artist, installation artist and Lecturer: http://nighthouse.withtank.com/

"A moment of Awareness occurred as I was walking down the street in San Francisco in the late 80's, when I suddenly realized that I essentially was the version of a motion picture hologram. In place of my desire to create a technology where light emanated from the source was life emanating from the source. The technology that I was interested in creating was essentially housed in all living things: I came to the conclusion that I no longer needed to concern myself with the externalized concept of motion picture holography. I began to refer to this realization as having swallowed myself whole.

This new awareness that I already had everything I needed alleviated the pressure to acquire sophisticated technologies. Simultaneously, I began to understand the concept of non-dualism in a significantly new way. It was a striking realization that changed my approach to seeing the world and became a major paradigm shift."

Aisling Burke, Actress, Ireland:
http://www.aislingburke.com/home.htm:

"Awareness to me is seeing life in a passionate and creative way. As an actress I develop my Awareness through performing and researching the lives of other characters. With this, I find out about the world around me. Also, through my parents, friends and family I have Awareness of the importance of health and happiness in life and enjoying each day."

Laura Canavan, Makeup Artist and Consultant and Director, Dublin:

"Simplicity. To close your eyes and take time to look inwards. To open with fresh eyes and a new perspective."

Declan Cassidy, Director, writer and founder of Timesnap Film and Media Productions: www.timesnap.com

"Awareness signifies my belief that I am a small but vital cog in the universal wheel of life."

Ali Coffey, Casting Director, Ireland:
www.fishpond.ie AND www.alicoffeycasting.ie,

"Awareness to me means valuing what and mainly who is important in your life and treasuring them accordingly. Awareness also means being present in the moment, which is something I constantly try and pull myself back to instead of racing ahead to the next thing."

Fainche Coffey, yogi, artist, health and fitness instructor and mother:

"Awareness is.... knowing the limitations of one's strengths and one's weaknesses and recognising that one's strength can become one's weakness if let go out of balance...
And thus identifying the equilibrium at which one can exist in one's optimum state...In harmony with one's self and one's environment."

Karen Costin, 5 Elements Acupuncturist, Ireland and International: http://www.karencostin.ie/

"Awareness is about the power of self-observation. By observing our thoughts and our feelings objectively we become more aware of how our thoughts reflect our reality."
Awareness is also about being open to all possibilities. I live by the philosophy that we create our own reality. Essentially, that we have the internal resources to heal, to create and to change our reality. It starts with connecting to the essence of our true selves. The journey starts with us learning to love ourselves. As a consequence of this process, love starts to come towards us in many different ways."

Stephen Cullen, Single dad and Salesman, Dublin:

"I see Awareness through my six year old daughter, who is the apple of my eye. I gain more Awareness each day through watching her grow up and being aware of her situation. She looks after me now as much as I look after her in this way."

John Devine, Natasha's dad, Director of coaching for the South Dublin football League: http://www.sdflsoccer.com/

"Awareness of one's self and the present moment is the key to serenity and calm."

Ken Devine, Dublin City Firefighter, Ireland:

"Awareness to me is described through a quote from the Dalai Lama and what surprises him about humanity 'because he sacrifices his health in order to make money. Then he sacrifices money to recuperate his health. He is so anxious about the future that he does not enjoy the present: the result being that he does not live in the present or the future: he lives as if he never going to die, and then dies having never really lived."

Debbie Devine, Urban Day Spa Owner:
http://www.urbandayspa.ie/

"Your task is not to seek for love, but merely to seek and find all the barriers within yourself that you have built against it." Jalal ad-Din Rumi quotes (Persian Poet and Mystic, 1207-1273)...
Awareness and Self-awareness is your perception of particular emotions or flows of energy. It is the body and mind connection, which can relax, calm and reduce stress and revitalize."

Danielle Rocca Devine, Marketing and Communications Specialist BNP PARIBAS Real Estate and Natasha's sister:

"Awareness to me is best described through my passion for music. Music is what feelings sound like to me. Music and the music industry allow me to live, meet and see the world through gigs, events and festivals all around the world. Music allows me to be fully present in the moment."

Richard Donelan, Executive Coach, Thinker and Athlete:
http://www.nextevolutioncoaching.com/

"Awareness is a trait which can assist us to pay closer attention to, and better observe, what's not going on and what's not being said. Quite often the loudest words can be spoken through silence or hidden by 'other' noise.

By being aware of this phenomenon we can become so much more tuned into what is truly being said and really happening around us.

Awareness is also about letting go of 'me'. This involves forgetting about our thoughts and our needs and instead focusing on what others need and really have to say.
We can achieve this goal by listening on a deeper level and focusing to ensure that we really hear what isn't being said.

In time we can build a much greater understanding of others around us and eventually this will lead to an awareness of their needs on a much deeper level. Until we make the effort to be more aware, who knows the value we might be able to add or what disaster we might be able to avert by practicing this belief."

Michael Doyle, Creative Director, Peter Mark Hair Salon Ireland; http://www.petermark.ie/

"For me, Awareness began through the loss of loved ones, which has made me treasure the gift of life. My working life as Creative Director allows me to gain more Awareness each day through my clients. I laugh with them, hear their good times, help them through their hard times and they do the same for me.

Recently, I had to shave the hair of a client. Of course it is hard for a female to loose her hair, but it was hard for me too. I cut her new wig, which made her feel like a beautiful woman. We laughed, we cried and embraced that moment together.

My advice is: be aware, we live, we die, but when we live never be afraid to laugh and to cry. When we live we should be honest and support each other. Laugh and cry together, never forget the bad times but always cherish the good times…then each day smile."

Robbie Doyle, Singer Song-writer, ex-professional footballer and newly qualified chef:

"I have gained my awareness through my family. From an early age family was always the strength that I needed to get by. They were always there for me in times if trouble and the good times too. It is only when you loose someone so close to you, like I did when my brother died at age of 27, that I gained Awareness and realized what a big part of my life they are.

From this loss, it was obvious what meaning family adds to my life on an everyday basis. Especially my father, who always reminded me while growing up of a quote he stood by that 'God did not give you dreams up order to taunt you, God gave you dreams in order for you to carry them out and succeed'. For me, without, my family, I'd have nothing."

Vanessa Matias Fahy, Irish Actress:
http://www.vanessamatiasfahy.com/

"Awareness to me means knowing that you are only one tiny jigsaw piece to the universe. We share this earth with millions of other creatures and we have to protect and honor the souls who have walked before us and those who will come after us. As individuals, we might only be a small fraction to the bigger picture but know that it takes only one person to make an impact. To know and believe every day that we can be more powerful than we ever thought possible is both frightening and empowering. Be aware that love and knowledge is power."

Aaron Farrell, Project Manager, Octagon Films, Ireland: www.octagonfilms.com

"Awareness is seeing things other people don't see at a speed other people don't see them at."

David Flanagan, Owner of 'David Flanagan Painting contractors' and Wado Ryu Boxer, Ireland:
http://www.davidflanagancontractors.ie/

"I have gained Awareness through my Wado Ryu training, which I have been doing for 18 years. Since I was a kid, one thing I will always remember is when you enter a dojo (training centre) you sweep and clean the floors. I never really knew the reason for this "ritual" or exercise until I got into the black belt ranks.

Yet, the idea is that you clean the floors to brush all your worries, anxieties and every other feeling, that day-to-day life has an effect on you. Here, you let go and and sweep them out of the dojo so you can immerse yourself fully physically and mentally into your training. Nothing else matters for the few hours but the training you do. It helps clear your mind and body and makes you aware of the important things around you."

Jonathon Forbes, Dublin City Firefighter, Ireland:

"Awareness is seeing past yourself. When 99% are running out of a burning building, 1% are running in, nor for money or fame, of the hope you may save someone's life without thinking you might lose yours."

Marian Gale: Fashion Boutique Owner, Dublin:
http://www.mariangale.ie/

"Awareness to me is all about the A's alert, alive and antennae turned on! When you stand behind a counter for the last 30 years as I have, you develop radar, a built in antennae and an acute awareness as to where people are.

One can pick up a vibe or awareness that all is ok or NOT ok with people you deal with. Awareness can also be an attitude, an attitude you choose to live your life by."

Glenn Gannon, Author, Playwright, Actor, Award winning short story writer, Ireland:
http://glenngannon.wordpress.com/

"Awareness is to put it quite simply is a knowing. It is the feeling inside oneself of a distinct difference between self and external forces of life. It is quite complex but the more I thought about it the simpler it became.

Self is not just a physical thing it is also a feeling living sensing thing that takes it at its most basic, *Rene Descartes* the philosopher I believe explained it best "I THINK THEREFORE I AM". I would add to that if I could, "I sense therefore I am aware". If I sense my awareness, then I am actively involved in it.

Therefore. I am producing my future in my mind because I sense my future before it happens. I say I have a feeling that today will bring good fortune or a variety of different things into my reality. So, my awareness tells me that I am in control. Hence, if I think positive, I am drawing positivity to me (like an unseen magnetic force draws a pin to a magnet). I feel my future before it happens, this to me is the ultimate example of a person who is completely self-aware."

Dean Gelis, Accountant and Singer/Songwriter, Ischia and Milan, Italy:

"La consapevolezza è di accettare che la mia anima è come un faro con attimi di buio e luce. E La mente è l'unico luogo dove ogni cosa può esistere realmente…

Awareness is to accept that my soul is like a lighthouse with moments of darkness and light. And the mind is the only place where anything can really exist."

Rich & Helene Guzman, LA ROX Inc., Personal Trainers Hollywood, California: http://larox.net/

"Our philosophy and focus has always been to bring balance to the mental, physical, emotional, and nutritional aspects of your life to create awareness. This is an attitude we instill through our teaching and our own lifestyle. Awareness is discovering your balance."

Robert Hartigan, Digital Compositor, Ireland: www.vimeo.com/user1323634

"Awareness for me in terms of work is attention to detail is everything. Working in feature film visual effects I thrive towards making the unbelievable believable, whether it's a futuristic space battle or reconstructing the titanic in the shipyards of Belfast."

Rebecca Hoover, Light Artist and Student, Boston: http://rehoover.tumblr.com/post/11938975562

"Awareness and consciousness go hand and hand. The world is about the relationships of matter in motion: always fluctuating, wavering, producing tensions that insight change. Our understanding of the world is based on our perception of those relationships.

Whether we acknowledge this consciously or subconsciously, our comprehension of this reality is often the definitive factor in our personal success.

Unfortunately, most of us live day to day with our eyes shut, completely oblivious to the nature of our own relationships and perceptions. It's only when we give ourselves the permission to absorb our experiences within full consciousness that we open ourselves up to opportunities for personal change and ingenuity.

There is nothing more valuable or more terrifying than allowing yourself to feel the full extent of your sensations: the warmth of light, the excitement of laughter, and the pain in reaching one's physical limits. A life without acknowledgement of these things is a life unworthy."

Jane Irvine CIP: Underwriter Commercial Team, Allianz:

"Awareness is an ability to fully embrace the present whilst never neglecting how we have been shaped by the past nor how we will impact on the future."

Thom Jordan Actor, Ireland:
http://www.facebook.com/pages/Thom-Jordan/169246509821806

"Awareness to me means watching many aspects of my life, from family & friends to the people I surround myself with on a daily basis.
Awareness for mental and physical health needs a sharp mind & I find with a conscious decision of balanced food and a rich personal life I can orientate myself in a far sharper manor which in turn leaves me with a much higher & prominent sense of awareness."

Brian Junior Kavanagh, Dad, Ireland:

"I find awareness through my religion because I'm a very spiritual person. My religion has helped me through some very hard times in life."

Treacy Kenny, Digital Media Consultant, Trader Media Group, Ireland: http://www.tradermediagroup.com/

"Awareness to me is having an open mind."

Emma Ledden, Creator of Presenting To Sell and Natasha's Communications coach, Ireland: http://www.presentingtosell.com/

"I believe we have the answers to all the questions we ask inside of us and awareness is being brave enough to listen to our truth."

Anne Leonard, Owner and Founder of Bikram Ireland: http://www.bikramyoga.ie/Welcome.html

"Awareness is being more concerned for those around you than for yourself."

David Mahony, guide for a 'Zipline Eco-tours' and Sustaining Communities, New Zealand and Laos: http://www.ziptrek.com/ AND http://www.sustainingcommunities.org/

"For me, I gain Awareness of myself, others and the world through sport.

Starting off, team sports enhance my awareness of my teammates and their strengths and weaknesses, as well as my opponents. This type of sport also increases your understanding of other countries and cultures when you follow or compete in these sports on an international level. Whereas, outdoor activities increase my self-awareness of my own abilities and give a greater degree of respect and understanding for the natural environment.

Overall in sports, when your abilities match your desired performance you experience a thing called "flow" where you are completely focused on the task at hand. It allows you to leave the other concerns of life. So, when you have finished you experience an increase in dopamine and endorphins in your brain which contribute to a greater sense of well being."

Caoilinn Taylor McGlade, Irish Model and Hotelier - Living in Goa:

"How you see yourself is most important - to be self assured and confident in your own skin. It means being satisfied with who you are, not always an easy task, and very easy to lose sight of yourself and what you stand for in times of trouble.

We reflect ourselves in others, and when I am happiest, I make others happy. During my modeling career, I have worked on myself to stay centered, as it is quite a harsh industry, without a strong head on ones shoulders I have seen too many girls get carried away with the craziness of dieting and worse, low confidence and putting themselves down-for what?
I have learnt to always be aware of the impact your words have on others - criticize softly, and praise very very loudly. Portraying positive energy wherever possible can be a blessing on others and essentially yourself."

Michelle Rocca Morrison, M.Phil. MA and Natasha's mum:

"Both our own lives and the world are going through such challenges at present that it is essential to our physical, emotional and mental health that we try to live every day with awareness and balance. We can then respond creatively in the moment to whatever life presents us.

The starting point for growth and healing is this moment. The key is our willingness to step back from a situation and accept it exactly as it is. We need to listen to the guidance of our true self (our intuition, our spirit) instead of acting out of the fear that comes from our ego (everyday identity, our personality).

The more aware we are the more prepared we are for change and growth. We can learn the lesson we need to learn in any given situation. We have the opportunity to reach our full potential in our career, relationship or wherever we choose.

Treacy O'Connor, EFT practitioner, Ireland:
http://www.facebook.com/treacyoconnor

"Awareness, for me, is the ability to tune into the part of yourself that is in alignment with the Divine source — a frequency of the highest vibration, and bring that alignment into full consciousness in our thoughts, words and actions-To live consciously and from the heart.

Most people are living unconsciously, driven by their subconscious mind, ego and head. When we experience the joy of conscious living, there are no more comments that we didn't really mean to say, actions that we didn't really mean to take, or thoughts that we have no control over. The ego will always fight for its survival in whatever way necessary and is often so subtle, that it is undetectable to each individual. Being aware, is the ability to detect this subtleness, always Questioning our motivation and intent and checking that we are aligning ourselves to the highest possible vibration and frequency for our own highest good and the highest good of all those around us.

When we are in that place of knowing, we accept that everyone is on an experiential journey and in order to reach a state of good awareness, each person has to pass through the challenges the ego presents us with. The ego however is not there to be destroyed; it must be embraced as part of who we are. It is there to show us balance, pointing us in the direction of our teachings, allowing us to be fully aware of our being — physical, emotional, spiritual and mental."

Patrick Peacocke, Cobbler, C and D Shoes, Dublin, Ireland:
http://www.cdshoes.ie/

"I find my Awareness through people in my life. I feel that there needs to be more awareness in health studies for disease prevention and cure, especially in terms of Motor Neuron disease."

Our awareness will constantly evolve and expand once we are willing to feel the initial discomfort required for change. Once we accept a situation we can choose in any given moment to act negatively out of ego or personality or to act creatively from our higher aware self and with the right motivation.

Morphing through difficult issues can affect our equilibrium, we may even go to extremes in behaviors, but staying in a place of awareness will help us regain balance and bring further clarity.

As we face our fears and blocks, we let go all our past and present issues and move forward to lead more fulfilled, balanced and creative lives. We rise above the mundane to see the bigger picture, the higher ground: we see things from our deeper reality with no fear, from a place of love, with no judgment or blame.

We can use our awareness to help evolve spiritually. We can also be a catalyst for healing those around us. In healing ourselves, we also help raise consciousness to a higher level and we become part of the collective healing of the planet."

Carlos Alonso-Niemeyer, LC, LEED AP, CEM: Program Manager for Energy Efficiency Services at NSTAR and Consultant at Alonso-Niemeyer Consulting Engineering Services: http://www.alonso-niemeyer.com/

"Awareness is the level of intensity to which I live my life. To be fully aware of everything that surrounds me and to enjoy life to the fullest."

Paula O'Connor, Psychotherapist and Metamorphosis Practitioner:

"Awareness to me is being in tune with your soul. When you speak with the voice of true self. It is the reward that comes with healing."

Frank Reen, Businessman, USA and Ireland:

"Where possible place yourself in other people's shoes in the hope that life can become clearer, a little easier to understand and infinitely more enjoyable!"

Alistair Reynolds, Consultant at The 'InVictus Group', London: www.invictusgroup.co.uk

"Self Awareness is one of the most difficult things to exemplify, yet, one of the most rewarding to discover. In my case, I am thankful to my friends and mentors who've helped me progress on my search."

Ann O'Riordan, Business lady, Healthcare, Ireland:

"Awareness is a sense of belonging, knowing where she fits, in order for her to move forward and deal with her reality."

Lisa Rocca, Mother of three, Lisbon:

"For me awareness is empathy, compassion, consideration and being patient. It's about seeing beyond the surface and having more insight into people and life in general."

Claudia Rocca Ryan: International Business student and sister to Natasha:

"Awareness is growth, and learning from life's trials and tribulations as they shape who you are. It is always remembering to laugh, as life without laughter is grey. Most importantly, not forgetting, sometimes in life, it is best to stop, don't talk and just dance."

Barend Slabbert, South African Interior architect and lecturer:

"Awareness is the ability to know that you can heal yourself. It is the process in which I make a constant decision to change my circumstances for the better, by focusing on aspects that enhance my life and shifting all negative energy out of it.

It is where I accept myself and come to terms with the fact that I can't change the past, but I can influence the future, so that I live with no regrets. So, living only with enthusiasm and optimism for the future ahead. Thus, healing starts when you have a goal you reach through determination, with motivation and a positive attitude."

Dr. Naomi Smith, Ireland:

"For me awareness is about paring ourselves back to our true core and letting go of the non essential things that can so easily fog up our minds. It's about finding time to understand the uniqueness of our own body and our mind.

To take a journey of self-discovery and find out whom you really are-: your likes and dislikes as well as your talents. Having an understanding of who you truly are leads to a sense of freedom and clarity which gives you the creativity, empowerment and confidence to move forward in life thus leading to happiness and fulfillment."

Robbie Smyth, Deputy Head, Faculty of Journalism and Media Communications, Griffith College, Dublin:
http://www.gcd.ie/

"Awareness is both an obligation and a privilege. We should be aware of our surroundings, ourselves, our wider social and individual personal circumstances, always understanding that this is for everyone a unique particular and solitary experience.

We cannot prescribe awareness. We can only recommend, encourage, facilitate and maybe even teach how to become aware. In full health, well educated and resource rich as we often are in wealthy states like Ireland we have an obligation to know. This awareness comes with an obligation to act, especially if we know others are being deprived of the lifestyle luxuries and political freedoms we enjoy day to day.

Being aware means to me to be awake in every sense of the world, to have the power to exert will and make conscious informed decisions. It is one of the unique aspects of human ability - to be consciously aware. It is also one of the hardest tasks to undertake, to be truly conscious and mindful of how we make our journey through this life."

Yoko Ota-Sawyer, Business lady, Boston:

"To live the moment with the open heart to accept who you are, the strength to face the reality, and the courage to go after what you believe."

Dr. Laura Toogood, Media Consultant, Journalist & Fashion Editor: www.lauratoogood.com AND www.thesloaney.com

"Awareness can be interpreted differently, but I believe it primarily concerns understanding how your behaviour impacts other people. Learning to be compassionate and to have empathy is very important."

Betsy Wagner, Realtor, Bushari Residential Real Estate, Boston: www.bushari.com

"Awareness can cover a broad range of facets in ones life. It can be awareness of self, of the world, of your immediate surroundings, or simply of nothing at all.

It is a word and a concept that is truly different to each person and its definition ebbs and flows based on each individual's character and personality. To me, awareness is everything. No matter the definition, without it we are lost in a self-absorption that can permeate every aspect of our lives. With it, we become influential, powerful and meaningful beyond belief.

My personal interpretation and implementation of "awareness", is *actively* perceiving how my beliefs, actions and words affect the people surrounding me. Whether it means smiling as I pass a stranger on the sidewalk, or speaking up when someone is uncomfortable as a result of other's actions, awareness is not just recognizing that it is happening but also acting in a transcendent manner.

When we act in a way that is different and in a way that takes into account the feelings and the happiness of others, it not only changes their life during that moment, but it also changes us as individuals and the perception others may have of us.

It changes who we are down to the very core. If we simply become Aware of how we can affect the happiness of those around us, and what we can do every day to simply respect that or even to grow it, our response becomes a personal habit. It becomes a personality. This interpretation of awareness also becomes memorable to all whom we meet, no matter how brief the encounter may be. It leaves an imprint on their day. It may make a permanent impact in their life.

Regardless of the result, the beauty of simply being aware in this manner, is that all you have to do is be active in your perception of how others feel, and respond with the goal of a smile. If you've accomplished just that, your simple awareness has made a difference."

AJ Williams, Owner of AJ Williams Events, Boston:
www.ajwilliamsevents.com

"I have overcome tragedy a few times in my life with a remarkable ability to persevere through life. To overcome tragedy I wanted to achieve something extraordinary – 10 years ago that was to launch a successful events company, AJ Williams Events.

Today, I create beautiful and press worthy event environments and it's the positive thinking that keeps my business and my personal life afloat. Positive thinking should be thought of as a technique that transforms you.

I have a favorite quote by Phillippe Venier "It's up to you to ILLUMINATE the world." The quote encourages you to shine your own light and bring your gifts to the world. No matter what you are faced with, no matter what life brings you – YOU create the path you desire and illuminate…

HERE'S TO YOUR SHINING LIGHT!"

MY SINCEREST THANKS...

◊ To my family, I must proceed with my individual 'Thanks':

◊ To John (dad), I thank you for your honesty and showing me the meaning of true love. I have never known a man to love and live his passions so profoundly: family and football.

◊ To Michelle (mum), Thank you for sharing with me ways to heal, communication and for always being honest. Most of all, for giving me the love and light of my sisters and brother.

◊ My Sisters, niece and brother I must give you all singular praise:
◊ To Danielle: Thank You for being stronger and more beautiful than you even realize. Also, for sharing with us my angel niece and goddaughter, Alanna.
◊ To Alanna, like your name and heart 'Álainn', you are beautiful.
◊ To Claudia, thank you for being angelic, yet, everyday so funny and such a light to my life in each day.
◊ To Éabha, thank you for being so sure and magical so young.
◊ To Fionn, fearless and equally magical, you melt my heart each day.

◊ To Van (stepdad) for sharing with me Awareness. ·

◊ To my remarkable grandparents: Maureen, Paddy and Eileen and late Jack.
◊ To my beautiful aunts: Paula, Lisa, Laura, Theresa, Annette, Debbie, Tina, Phyllis... and many more.
◊ To my uncles: Especially to the late Patrick and Christy.
◊ To my cousins and extended family-you are all part of my strength, ESPECIALLY THE CHILDREN... YOU ARE ALL ANGELS.

◊ To Cillian and Danielle Ryan and all members of the Ryan family.

◊ To John Morris for my fantastic website and your belief in me: www.awarenessinlife.com

MY SINCEREST THANKS...

◊ To EACH of the book's contributors and EACH PERSON QUOTED. I am so grateful for your help in creating 'AWARENESS'-GRAZIE!

◊ Thank you to Mollie Harrison, Jennifer Slaybaugh, Gregory Eckart and all those at 'Balboa Press-Hay House' and my PR team. Each for their guidance and enthusiasm, especially Adriane Pontecorvo-you are a star!

◊ Thank you to Megumi Mizuno for her nail art seen in the 'Imagination' image: http://www.facebook.com/megumi.mizuno

◊ Thank you endlessly to my 'Awareness' lawyer Kevin O' Leary, from 'Coughlinbetke Boston' for your advice, help and belief: http://www.coughlinbetke.com/KJO.html

◊ To all my close friends, 'my tribe' or 'famiglia": Jane I, Gemma H, Lauren T, Alistair R, Robbie D, Meg M, Sonje G, Naomi S, Foteini, Claire S, Maeve O'S, Steven D, Barend S, Aisling B, Aoife R, Laura C, Yare, Laura T, Siobhan G, Frank R, Sophie B, Arabella B, Alexandre R, Alice F, Bettina, Ian K, Nicholas T, Adamo M,... and more. Thank you each one.

◊ To the Rafter, Irvine, Bushell, Murphy and Scally families-Thank you always for your kindness.

◊ To Margaret and Emma Boland, who both changed my life through sharing with me the practice of Metamorphosis: http://www.metamorphosis-rstjohn.com/

◊ To my parents, uncle Patrick, aunts Lisa, Paula and Debbie, Along with Declan Cassidy, Emma Ledden, Joan Mulvihill and Robert Hartigan, for being my career mentors. Thank you all.

◊ To Caroline Morson:'The Morson Collection': http://themorsoncollection.com/ who inspires me greatly. I thank you endlessly for your belief and support in me. To both you and your daughters, Taylor and Brooke, for being such beautiful souls and for living life with class, style and always with a smile.

MY SINCEREST THANKS…

◊ Brian O'Neill Jnr, Immigration Lawyer Boston:
  http://www.btolaw.com/, for taking your job to another level,
  in your ability to help others (who are passionate about
  sharing their skills in America), to have a chance to do so,
  myself included. You are a remarkable man.

◊ To John Mansfield, Boston Valet: http://www.bostonvalet.com/
  You embody the label of a 'cool saint'.

◊ To Richard and George (Sagarino's owners Boston), and Alison
  and Barbara, for being fantastic, funny and kind!

◊ To Rebecca Weir, 'Light IQ' London, for inspiring me through
  her lectures to follow my passion and specialise in lighting
  design. Along with, Philip Moule and Roberto Serra for giving
  me the opportunity to work with each one and such a fantastic
  team in 'Light IQ' firm London:
  http://www.lightiq.com/about.php

◊ To Light Engineer, LC, LEED AP, CEM: Programme Manager at N-
  Star and consultant, Carlos Alonso Niemeyer: http://alonso-
  niemeyer.com/

◊ AND Light Installation and Light Artist Elaine Buckholtz:
  http://nighthouse.withtank.com/ For both sharing with me the
  'Power of Light'.

◊ To Michael Barsky, my most wonderful landlord in Boston...
◊ All the staff at 'CINNAMON CAFÉ' Ranelagh Dublin...
◊ And of course my sister Danielle, for each allowing me
  space to write and create 'AWARENESS'- THANK YOU!!!

◊ For my Photo shoot: To the photographer.

◊ To Travis Rutzel and Jill Ferguson at 'Rock, Paper, Scissors'
  hair salon in Boston; http://rpssalon.com/

◊ To Ashely Shakespeare, Make up Artist at Sephora in The
  Prudential, Boston; http://www.sephora.com/

MY SINCEREST THANKS...

◊ To all my friends and tutors in each school and college that I have studied or practiced in. THANK YOU ALL...

◊ Especially my sports coach Mr. C and my Art teacher Ms. Murphy (Alexandra College Dublin)

◊ And Ellisavet Botsi and Hugo (KLC School of Design, London).

◊ To Ben Glassner (Boston), for being 'Aware' beyond your years. I can already see your name in bright lights: http://www.trendarazzi.com/

◊ To Alla Svirinskaya for sharing with me the power of Energy: http://www.allasvirinskaya.com/

◊ To Adam and the teams in Blueprint printers, Dublin: http://www.blueprint.ie/flashsite/index.htm

◊ To Oprah and Ellen DeGeneres, Thank you both for representing an idea of honesty, humour and shining light on and to the world.
Most of all, giving hope and happiness to people and children in need.

THANK YOU TO EACH PERSON I HAVE MET TO DATE.
YOU HAVE EACH GIVEN ME AWARENESS...
WISHING YOU ALL HAPPINESS AND LIGHT.
NRD.

AWARENESS...

IT'S NOT HOW
BIG YOU ARE,
IT'S HOW BIG
YOU PLAY

*Typography and Graphics: NRD

Abundance

If you take note of all that is around you and all the people in your life, you will see that there is limitless abundance available.

"Riches are not from abundance of worldly goods but from a contented mind." Mohammed

"Not what we have but what we enjoy constitutes our abundance." Epicurus

ACCEPTANCE

ACCEPT YOU. ACCEPT OTHERS. ACCEPT NOW.

ACKNOWLEDGEMENT

Please acknowledge yourself and others; even a simple smile could lighten up someone's day.

"Acknowledgement of one another's faults is the highest duty imposed by our love of truth." Ambrose Bierce

"Some of the most devastating things that happen to you will teach you the most." Ellen DeGeneres

ACTING AND HEALING

Having studied and practiced in acting both on stage and camera, I experienced the healing qualities that it encompasses. Not only is acting creative as it embodies the idea of living in the moment, but also it broadened my Awareness of others.

Yet, each day, I see people all around the world showing Oscar-worthy performances.
In order to protect themselves in life, people embody a role pending on which environment they are placed in.

*NEW IDEA:
STOP ACTING IN LIFE.

Take a class in ACTING and performance but keep DRAMA for the stage or Film Set. BEING TRUE TO YOURSELF in every moment is the key to happiness. NRD

"I have a holistic need to work and to have huge ties of love in my life. I can't imagine eschewing one for the other." Meryl Streep

"The actor should be able to create the universe in the palm of his hand." Sir Laurence Olivier

"True actors don't just *want* to act: you are compelled to this life. It is a life vocation that breathes through your veins and no other life will do. I am blessed to know what I want to do for the rest of my life, not everyone is that lucky. Acting lives in the imagination and is self-healing! It inspires me every day to be the best person I can be.

You experience roles that are wonderful and some that are tormenting and sad and that has left me with empathy and compassion for all that I experience in my own life.

Whatever I may be going through in my own life on any given day - when I walk into a rehearsal room, or on stage or on set, that gets left behind at the door and I play - I play with truth, honesty and integrity and the dream is that my dedication gives someone watching the escapism and inspiration they are seeking."
Irish Actress Vanessa Mathias Fahy

ACTION

I agree with Robert St John (Metamorphosis) that 'the mind behind the action is the beginning of everything'. Action is necessary to gain results. Yet, in order for things to be creative, it must begin from a place of balance.

IF YOU WISH FOR CREATIVE RESULTS… BE HONEST AND ACT ONLY ON YOUR INSTINCTS. nrd

"One must learn by doing the thing, for though you think you know it, you have no certainty until you try." Aristotle

"Every action has an equal and opposite reaction."
Sir Isaac Newton

"IF YOU DONT BACK IT UP WITH PERFORMANCE AND HARD WORK... TALKING DOESN'T MEAN A THING." MICHAEL JORDAN

ACUPUNCTURE

I have tried Acupuncture various times, which I felt helped my circulation and grounded me after each treatment. In this treatment it deals with the symptom of your imbalance.

According to the Acupuncture Council of Ireland: "The traditional Chinese theory holds that the body's life energy called Qi (pronounced Chee) travels around the body in pathways called meridians. The acupuncturist views illness as an energetic imbalance and is able to influence this imbalance by inserting very fine needles at certain points along these channels called Acupoints.

The acupuncturist may also use heat treatment (called Moxibustion) or Cupping in the treatment."

NOTE: CUPPING IS USED AS A MEANS OF DETOXIFYING THE BODY. PREPARE FOR IMMEDIATE BRUSING. SO, PLEASE DO NOT PLAN ANY BEACH TRIPS POST-CUPPING!

ACUPRESSURE

Acupressure is suggested for those who are fearful of needles and can be used during and after treatments. It applies the same fundamentals as Acupuncture.

Acupressure stimulates the same points along the meridians as acupuncture without the use of needles. This can be performed by the patient at home and is often used on very young children both at home and in a clinic setting.

AFFECTION

Affection is part of life. **EMBRACE AFFECTION.**

"We can live without religion and meditation, but we cannot survive without human affection." Dalai Lama

ALIVENESS

*EXERCISE:
FIND AN ACTIVITY THAT MAKES YOU FEEL ALIVE and IN THE MOMENT.

"Don't worry about what the world needs. Ask yourself what makes you come alive and do that. What the world needs is people who have come alive." Dr. Howard Thurman

"THERE'S A FIRE STARTING IN MY HEART...REACHING A FEVER PITCH AND ITS BRINGING ME OUT OF THE DARK." ADELE

BE THE BEST YOU CAN BE.
EACH MOMENT YOU SHOULD AND DESERVE TO SHINE. Nrd

"Your soul's purpose is to participate in wholeness: to express love, delight, joy, creativity and all of those qualities that emerge from Source, from wholeness." HIRO BOGA

We ask ourselves, "Who am I to be brilliant, gorgeous, talented and fabulous? Actually, who are you not to be?" Marianne Williamson

ANGER

ANGER =
INNER FREEDOM CHALLENGED
*PLEASE RELEASE THIS AS WITH ANGER ONLY YOU LOSE. NRD

"Whenever you are confronted with an opponent, conquer him with love." Mahatma Gandhi

ANIMALS

Animals are natural healers as they are representative and connected to growth and nature.

"UNTIL ONE HAS LOVED AN ANIMAL, A PART OF ONE'S SOUL REMAINS UNTOUCHED."
ANTOLE FRANCE

TO DO: Spend time outdoors either walking your dog, or your neighbours (please ask first ☺) or visiting the local zoo or park. Animals and nature will make you smile and ground you in that moment.

"Our task must be to free ourselves... by widening our circle of compassion to embrace all living creatures and the whole of nature and its beauty." Albert Einstein

ANGELS

Whether you believe in angels or not, I embrace their concept, which is of seeing creation and light in life. Like Michelangelo says; "I saw an Angel in the marble and carved until I set it free."

ART AND HEALING

In my opinion art and healing are symbiotic. I disagree with the idea that creating drama or pain to create art is necessary. Also, disagreeing with the concept that artists should be stereotyped as victims. True artists are messengers recording a moment in time in a creative way.

PAIN=PAIN.
CREATION=CREATION.

Hence, Art must be created in a moment of creativity. It then allows people to channel their passion and pain into something creative. Therefore, art is a way to heal, whilst creating something beautiful.

*Q and A: We all have artistic qualities, what are yours?

"Love the art in yourself, not yourself in the art."
Konstantin Stanislavsky

"All true artists, whether they know it or not, create from a place of no-mind, from inner stillness." Eckhart Tolle

"Artists are visionaries. We routinely practice a form of faith, seeing clearly and moving toward a creative goal that shimmers in the distance- often visible to us but invisible to those around us." Julia Cameron

ATTITUDE

Your attitude in each day is reflective of your state of mind. People who have respect and pride for their job, life and others have the right attitude.
IF YOU HAVE A NEGATIVE ATTITUDE THEN PLEASE WORK ON IT NOW! REMEMBER, IT IS DOWN TO YOU TO CHANGE IT.
EVERYONE AROUND YOU DESERVES TO BE HAPPY.
YOU DESERVE TO BE HAPPY.

"If you can do something about a bad situation, why be angry about it? Just do it! If you can't do anything about it, why hurt yourself more by getting angry about it?

Frustration is the fuel of bitterness and anger. Remain cheerful and you stay free, no matter what happens, life or death."
Shantidera, great Indian Buddhist sage

AROMATHERAPY:

Aromatherapy is where Essential oils from plants are used and massaged onto the skin. The oils are noted to stimulate the brain and therefore have a relaxing effect to calm you in that moment.

ASTROLOGY

THERE IS ASTROLOGY AND CHINESE ASTROLOGY. BOTH INDICATING THAT THE MOMENT THAT YOU ARE BORN; (THE MONTH AND YEAR) CAN TYPIFY CERTAIN TRAITS IN YOUR PERSONALITY.
IN ASTROLOGICAL TERMS, IT IS SUGGESTED THAT EACH MONTH AND YEAR HAD UNIQUE ELEMENTS OF WHERE THE PLANETS ETC. WERE ALIGNED. SO, PEOPLE BORN IN THE SAME MONTH ARE SAID TO SHARE THE SAME STARSIGN AND VARIOUS TRAITS.

THESE SIGNS ARE SUGGESTED TO HELP DESCRIBE YOU AND ALLOW YOU TO UNDERSTAND YOUR PERSONAL TRAITS. AND FOR YOU TO UNDERSTAND OTHERS PERSONALITIES THROUGH THEIR ASTROLOGICAL OR CHINESE SIGNS…

"We are born at a given moment in a given place and like vintage years of wine we have the qualities of the year and of the season in which we are born. Astrology does not lay claim to anything else." Carl G. Jung

AURA SOMA

In Aura Soma treatments, you chose an Aura Soma bottle, of a variety of colours in every visit. The one you chose represents the area or block that you need to re-balance at that point in time. From this, you work through this block through colour, scents and vibrational methods of healing.

According to www.thecolourrose.com, as a universal language, color expresses part of the universe's underlying order and rhythm. Aura-Soma uses the visual and non visual energy of color, the energies of herbs from essential oils and herbal extracts and the energies of crystals and gems. It helps develop greater awareness of our life purpose, gifts, talents and challenges.

AWARENESS

Awareness is an abstract idea. Some see it as ENLIGHTENMENT, AWAKENING… etc. which is exciting as each person shares a unique idea on this. Through Metamorphosis and life experience I have broadened my Awareness on a deeper level, which also allows me to understand the idea on a practical level. I believe it must begin within to understand Awareness outside of yourself. Living in the moment and in balance allows awareness and balance to happen each day.

The New Webster's Dictionary and Thesaurus defines aware as: "conscious, informed."

"3 things are absolute and cannot be destroyed: awareness, being and love." Deepak Chopra

Balance

Balance is the closest definition to 'perfection' in my eyes. It is down to you and I to base our decisions on balance in each day. Even if you go off balance, which is part of life. With 'Awareness' it is easier to get back on track. NO ONE IS PERFECT. WE ALL GO OFF BALANCE. EMBRACE IT. BALANCE IS ABOUT FINDING YOUR HAPPY MEDIUM IN EACH DAY.

"HAPPINESS IS NOT A MATTER OF INTENSITY, BUT OF BALANCE, RHYTHM AND HARMONY."
THOMAS MERTON

"An arch is two weaknesses which together make a strength."
Leonardo da Vinci

BEAUTY

"There is no excellent beauty that hath not some strangeness in the proportion." Francis Bacon

"Beauty is only skin deep. I think what's really important is finding a balance of mind, body and spirit." Jennifer Lopez

"The best and most beautiful things in the world cannot be seen, nor touched...but are felt in the heart." Helen Keller (1880-1968)

"There is nothing beautiful about creating the 'image of beauty'. Being happy in yourself in every moment, that is true beauty."

Natasha Rocca Devine

BE YOU.
YOU=BEAUTY.
BEAUTY=YOUR UNIQUENESS.NRD

BLOCKS

"Deep within us is a center, a nucleus, from which we have the potential of complete and absolute intelligence and functional ability. This nucleus is the individual consciousness. The principle of Metamorphosis is the ability to be able to "tune in" to this center in the ordinary practice of life. We don't use much of it because we are a mass of diversionary blocks."
Robert St. John, Metamorphosis

BODY

A healthy mind=healthy body +
A balanced mind=balanced body.

Yet, we are all built of different shapes and sizes. Embrace yours.
Eat well. Eat balanced.
Eat what your body desires in the moment.
*Always treat yourself and NEVER be scared to eat dessert first! NRD

BOUNDARIES

WITH TECHNOLOGY, THE WORLD
HAS NEVER BEEN SO CONNECTED.
COMMUNICATION IS SO EASY. AT
ANY MOMENT, PEOPLE CAN
INTERACT WITH FRIENDS ACROSS
THE WORLD, WITH A PARTNER WHO
WORKS OR LIVES ABROAD AND
EVEN WITH CLIENTS. TECHNOLOGY
ALLOWS PEOPLE TO CONTINUE
CLOSE FRIENDSHIPS, MAINTAIN
RELATIONSHIPS AND EVEN BUILD
A COMPANY FROM THEIR HOME.

*IN INTIMATE RELATIONSHIPS,
IF MISUSED TECHNOLOGY CAN
MAKE RELATIONS DISCONNECTED.
  • EACH DAY THROUGH TECHNOLOGY MANY
    ARE KEEPING SECRETS OR
    DISCONNECTING FROM THEIR
    RELATIONSHIPS BY SHARING THEIR
    ENERGY TO/WITH OTHERS (OTHER THAN
    THEIR PARTNER).

- MOST WITHOUT REALISING.
- ENERGY EXCHANGED IS VERY POWERFUL.
- SO, IN A MOMENT OF TRUTH:
- Q. WOULD YOU BE OPEN FOR YOUR PARTNER TO HEAR WHAT YOU SAY TO OTHERS?
- Q. TO SEE HOW YOU ACT WITH OTHERS?
- Q. TO READ TEXTS OR EMAILS YOU SEND TO/AND FROM THE OPPOSITE
- (OR SAME SEX-WHATEVER YOUR PREFERENCE)?
- Q. VIEW WHAT YOU VIEW ONLINE?
  LET'S SEE…
- Q. IF THE ROLES WERE REVERSED AND IT WAS YOUR PARTNER KEEPING SECRETS OR SHARING ENERGY WITH SOMEONE (S) OTHER THAN YOU,
- WOULD YOU BE HAPPY?

- A. TO ANSWER: IF YOU WALKED INTO A BAR/RESTAURANT TO SEE YOUR PARTNER WITH SOMEONE ELSE, WOULD YOU ACCEPT THIS?
- A. NO WAY.
- SO, WHY WOULD YOU SHARE THEM OR THINK ITS FAIR TO SHARE YOUR ENERGY WITH OTHERS THROUGH TECHNOLOGY?

- FACTS:
- SECRETS=NEGATIVE ENERGY=CHAOS.
- EACH ACTION HAS A REACTION.
- NEGATIVE REACTION=EVERYONE LOSES!
- IF YOU NEED ATTENTION, EVEN NEGATIVE, THEN ASK YOURSELF WHY?
- PERHAPS THAT IS THE PROBLEM.
- TRY CHANNELING IT INTO SOMETHING CREATIVE AND YOU WILL SEE POSITIVE RESULTS.

- EVEN WHEN APART OR ONLINE; IN TEXTS, EMAILS, AND IN ACTION, HOW YOU ACT, REPRESENTS BOTH YOU AND THEM ALIKE.
- SO, BE A STRONG TEAM!
- PLEASE BE CONFIDENT AND STRONG ENOUGH IN YOURSELF AND YOUR RELATIONSHIP TO FOCUS ON THAT AND ENJOYING IT.
- INSTEAD, USE YOUR ENERGY FOR EACH OTHER AND TO CREATE HAPPINESS EACH DAY OR FOR YOURSELF.

BE YOU. BE HONEST.
-EVEN EARLY ON IN RELATIONSHIPS,
 IF YOUR PARTNER DOESN'T ACCEPT
 YOUR BOUNDARIES PLEASE LET THEM GO!-

REMEMBER, YOU MUST DECIDE...

- TO BE HAPPY IN YOUR LIFE.
- TO BE HAPPY WITH WHAT YOU HAVE AND PROTECT THIS.
- TO RESPECT YOUR RELATIONSHIP.
- THAT RELATIONSHIPS COUNT ALL DAY/ EVERY DAY-
- YOU ARE ON THE SAME TEAM.
- NOT JUST AT A DINNER ONCE A WEEK!
- THAT YOU DESERVE AND WILL BE NUMBER 1 IN SOMEONES LIFE! EQUALLY, THEY DESERVE TO BE YOUR NUMBER 1! NEVER SETTLE!

PLEASE ONLY CREATE A RELATIONSHIP THAT WILL ENHANCE YOUR LIFE- NOT LIMIT. THEY ARE MEANT TO BE FUN! RESPECT OTHERS RELATIONSHIPS TOO.

MOST OF ALL,
REPSECT YOURSELF-N.R.D.

TASK: BE YOUR OWN 'SUPERHERO':
EACH DAY, EXPECT AND GIVE RESPECT.
HAVE RESPECT FOR YOURSELF.
HAVE RESPECT FOR OTHERS.
CREATE BOUNDARIES.
RESPECT BOUNDARIES.

BOUNDARIES=RESPECT=BALANCE= POSITIVITY=CREATIVITY=HAPPINESS= MORE TIME TO ENJOY LIFE! NATASHA RD

BREATH

REMEMBERING HOW TO BREATH IS ESSENTIAL.
THERE ARE MANY PRACTICES AROUND THE WORLD TO
SHOW YOU THIS; YOGA, MEDITATION ETC.
IN STRESSFUL SITUATIONS PEOPLE LOSE THIS NATURAL
ACTION AND MOVE INTO PANIC.
TASK: IN STRESSFUL MOMENTS, TAKE A FEW DEEP
BREATHS, FIND BALANCE AND GET BACK INTO THE MOMENT…
YOU ARE STRONG. BREATH AND LET GO... BE PRESENT.

"Breathe. Let go. And remind yourself that this very moment is the only one you know you have for sure."

Oprah Winfrey

"If you woke up breathing, congratulations! You have another chance." Andrea Boydston

C ARE

"Things done well and with a care, exempt themselves from fear." **William Shakespeare**

CHALLENGES

Challenges are part of daily life. For each person it differs. Whether it is remaining calm in traffic, overcoming obstacles in work or finding a balance between work and life outside. For you, a challenge may seem big, but not to others.
- SO, YOU ARE ENTITLED TO FEEL CHALLENGED.
- YET, All you must remember is: YOU CAN AND WILL OVERCOME THESE CHALLENGES:
- PRACTICE A METAMORPHOSIS HAND SYMBOL.
- WRITE IT DOWN.
- RUN IT OUT.
- SPEAK IT OUT.
- REMEMBER YOU ARE STRONG ENOUGH.
- BELIEVE IN YOURSELF AND YOUR STRENGTH.
- BELIEVE IN YOUR BALANCE.
- BELIEVE IN LIVING FOR TODAY. NRD

CHANGE

CHANGE IS INEVITABLE. It must begin with a decision to **allow for changes in yourself each day**. Allow your ideas, yourself and others to evolve and change in each moment. You will see magic come to life... NRD

CHARACTER

"When the character of a man is not clear to you, look at his friends." Japanese proverb

Character is a French word- 'caractere' meaning imprint on the soul. "Character is revealed when our mask is removed."

CHERISH

CHERISH YOUR INNER CHILD. NATASHA RD

"CHERISH YOUR HEALTH." NRD

CHILDREN

CHILDREN ARE RAYS OF LIGHT. THEY ARE HOPE.
EACH ONE DESERVES A CHANCE TO SHINE.

"Every child is an artist.
The problem is how to remain
an artist once we grow up."
Pablo Picasso

"There is nothing more thrilling in this world, I think, than having a child that is yours, and yet is mysteriously a stranger." **Agatha Christie**

"Children are the living messages we send to a time we will not see." John W. Whitehead, founder, Rutherford Institute

CHIROPRACTIC

"The nervous system holds the key to the body's incredible potential to heal itself." Sir Jay Holder, M.D., D.C., Ph.D., of Miami, Florida

"Many internal diseases are cured by the spinal adjustment alone. Leaving the adjustment (chiropractic) out of the treatment plan invites failure." Felix Mann, MD, Paul Nagler, MD and Kungo Magayama MD

CHOICE

CHOOSE BALANCE. NRD

"You are at choice always and in all ways." Neale Donald Walsch,

CLARITY

MAKE THINGS CLEAR IN LIFE. WE ALL HAVE OUR OWN IDEAS, SO YOU MUST BE CONCISE WITH YOURSELF AND PEOPLE YOU INTERACT WITH.

COMMUNICATION

COMMUNICATION IS ESSENTIAL IN:
- LIFE, LOVE AND BALANCE.
- COMMUNICATION IS SPEECH.
- COMMUNICATION IS WRITING.

- COMMUNICATION IS ART.
- COMMUNICATION IS BUSINESS.
- COMMUNICATION IS SPORT.
- COMMUNICATION IS TECHNOLOGY.
- COMMUNICATION IS HEALING.
- COMMUNICATION IS BODY LANGUAGE.
- COMMUNICATION IS HOW YOU DRESS (By 'not caring' you are caring, it is thought out).
- EVEN NON-COMMUNICATION IS COMMUNICATION (Ignoring someone is still energy shared and sending a message).

- TASK: OBSERVE HOW YOU ARE ALWAYS COMMUNICATING AND WHAT MESSAGES YOU ARE SHARING?
- *DO YOU REALISE THE POWER IN YOUR COMMUNICATION?!
- *BE HONEST IN COMMUNICATION.
- *SAY WHAT YOU HAVE TO SAY OR DETACH BUT DON'T PLAY GAMES.
- KEEP IN BALANCE…
- KEEP COMMUNICATION OPEN!

"Everything we say signifies: everything counts, that we put out into the world. It impacts on kids: it impacts on the zeitgeist of the time." **Meryl Streep**

"Communication is the key to balance in life. It connects people. Especially in times of chaos in life it is the medium to create solutions.

In my case, I am aware of the power of communication through my mothers' career as a television Broadcaster and my career in Communications alike.

Communication is my essence. Envisaging whom I am communicating with, for or to is the indicator in how to relay this message. Yet, to be successful in anything, you must always speak from a place of balance and truth." NATASHA RD

COMPASSION

"You are the people who are shaping a better world.
One of the secrets of inner peace is the practice of compassion." Dalai Lama

"Our sorrows and wounds are healed only when we touch them with compassion." Buddha

CONSCIOUSNESS

WHETHER YOU ARE CONSCIOUS OF THIS OR NOT:
YOU ALONE CAN MAKE A DIFFERENCE.

"The aim of Metamorphosis is to create balance and stability. It brings about freedom from negative unconscious memory and genetic influences out of the past." Margaret Boland, Metamorphosis practitioner, Ireland.

COOKING

For myself , cooking is about connecting people and embracing a special moment together. Cooking is also extremely creative and calming as it brings you into the moment. Followed by an even better moment: EATING!

TASK: TAKE A COOKING CLASS, COOK WITH AND FOR YOUR PARTNER, KIDS, FAMILY AND FRIENDS. IT IS A WAY TO CONNECT AND CHERISH THE SPECIAL PEOPLE IN YOUR LIFE. NRD.

"Bring the same consideration to the preparation of your food as you devote to your appearance. Let your dinner be a poem, like your dress." Charles Pierre Monselet, French journalist

"Cooking is like love, it should be entered into with abandon or not at all." Harriet Van Horne, Vogue 10/1956

COMMITMENT

"Starting something is easy, maintenance is where true commitment lies. Always remain balanced when you commit in life, especially in love." NRD

CONFIDENCE

- CONFIDENCE IS BEING TRUE TO YOURSELF AND YOUR VALUES EACH DAY.
- CONFIDENCE IS NOT ARROGANCE, EGO OR HURTING OTHERS TO 'BE THE BEST'.

- YET, YOU SHOULD NEVER PLAY IT SAFE OR DUMB YOURSELF DOWN TO MAKE OTHERS FEEL BETTER OR TO 'FIT IN'.
- HAVE THE CONFIDENCE TO BE YOU- WHICH IS BEING YOUR BEST IN EVERY MOMENT!
- EQUALLY, HAVE THE CONFIDENCE TO BE INSPIRED AND HAPPY FOR THOSE WHO ALSO HAVE CONFIDENCE.
- THIS WILL GIVE OTHERS THE CONFIDENCE TO BE THEIR BEST- TO BE THEMSELVES IN EVERY MOMENT.
- THE RIGHT PEOPLE WILL EMBRACE YOUR CONFIDENCE... THE OTHERS WILL CATCH UP... GO FIRST.
- LET YOURSELF SHINE.
- LET EVERYONE AROUND YOU SHINE.

TASK: CREATE CONFIDENCE! NRD

"Confidence is the most important single factor in this game, and no matter how great your natural talent, there is only one way to obtain and sustain it: work." Jack Nicklaus, American professional golfer

IF YOU DON'T BELIEVE IN YOURSELF, HOW DO YOU EXPECT OTHERS TO? START NOW. NRD

CONNECTION

- ◊ WE ARE ALL CONNECTED.
- ◊ TECHNOLOGY HAS GIVEN US A NEW WAY TO LIVE AND INTERACT.
- ◊ SO, ONE PERSONS MOVE OR ACTION WILL INEVITABLY AFFECT MANY AND THAT PERSON WILL AFFECT MANY MORE.
- ◊ CONNECTION WHEN USED POSITIVELY CAN CREATE A RIPPLE EFFECT ON THE WORLD...

- ◊ WHY DON'T YOU CONNECT TO OTHERS – ONLINE AND OFFLINE-BY SHARING YOUR TALENTS?
- ◊ SHOW THE WORLD YOUR SPECIAL LIGHT.
- ◊ SHARING YOUR TALENTS, YOU CAN BE THE PERSON OF POSITIVE CHANGE.

- ◊ DON'T WAIT FOR SOMEONE TO SHOW YOU,
- ◊ TAKE THE LEAD...
- ◊ WHAT ARE YOU WAITING FOR?" NRD

"I believe that two people are connected at the heart and it doesn't matter what you do, or who you are or where you live: there are no boundaries or barriers if two people are destined to be together." Julia Roberts

"Connection gives purpose and meaning to our lives." Brene Brown

CLOSENESS HAS NOTHING TO DO WITH DISTANCE.

WE ARE ALL CONNECTED.

IT IS THE SPACE IN BETWEEN THAT COUNTS IN RELATIONSHIPS.

KEEP CLOSE. KEEP CONNECTED. NATASHA ROCCA DEVINE

COURAGE

It takes courage to change. It is not always easy to overcome your blocks and fears… Yet, the results are always worth it. You are worth it! NRD

"I learned that courage was not the absence of fear, but the triumph over it. The brave man is not he who does not feel afraid, but he who conquers that fear." Nelson Mandela

"To awaken is an act of courage." Judith Orloff, MD

"Healing takes courage and we all have courage, even if we have to dig a little to find it." Tori Amos

"Failure is unimportant. It takes courage to make a fool of yourself." Charlie Chaplin

CREATIVITY

"My Creativity is derived from the balance between thought and action, at this moment is where the magic happens."
Natasha Rocca Devine

"Mystery is at the heart of creativity. That, and surprise." Julia Cameron

"Creativity is just connecting things. When you ask creative people how they did something, they just saw something. It seemed obvious to them after a while. That's because they were able to connect experiences they've had and synthesize new things." Steve Jobs

"One of the things that kept me out of trouble was doing something creative - creativity can't be judged." Beyoncé

Dance

Dancing for me is an art, which connects the past and present and allows creativity for the future. Dance is magical as it allows creativity to come to life in a set of unique moments=a show.
IT IS ALSO A FANTASTIC WAY TO HAVE FUN, EXERCISE AND ENJOY THE MOMENT.

"DANCERS ARE THE INSTRUMENTS LIKE A PIANO THE CHOREOGRAPHER PLAYS."
GEORGE BALANCHINE

"Dance first.
Think later.
It's the natural order."
Samuel Beckett

DECISIONS

EACH DAY WE MAKE DECISIONS WHICH SHAPE OUR DAY AND AFFECT THE DIRECTION THAT OUR FUTURE WILL TAKE (AND ALL THOSE IN OUR LIVES).

*PLEASE CONSIDER THE INTENTION OF ALL YOUR DECISIONS:

DECIDE TO CUT THE DRAMA.

DECIDE HAPPINESS.

DECIDE TO LIVE IN THE MOMENT.

DECIDE TO GIVE AND TAKE NOTHING LESS THAN WHAT YOU DESERVE IN EACH DAY AND IN EACH MOMENT.

"No one can make you feel inferior without your consent."

Eleanor Roosevelt (1884-1962)

DESIRE

NOWADAYS, THE WORLD IS FILLED WITH MANY OPTIONS...

- YET, OFTEN TOO MANY AND PEOPLE ARE LEFT OVERWHELMED.
- WITH OPTIONS, DESIRES HAVE INCREASED WORLDWIDE.
- *DESIRE IS NOW CONFUSED WITH CONSTANT PLEASURE
- AND INSTANT GRATIFICATION...
- PEOPLE MISS OUT ON RELATIONSHIPS, FRIENDSHIPS, FAMILY, HAPPINESS AND BALANCE.

- THEY MISS OUT ON NOW.
- EVERYONE HAS DESIRES AND PASSIONS, BUT SOME ARE DESTRUCTIVE TO THEIR LIVES, HEALTH AND ALSO THOSE IN THEIR LIVES. ONLY THEY KNOW THE TRUTH IN THIS.
- *QUICK-FIXES IN ALL ASPECTS OF LIFE DON'T LAST AND ARE ALL BASED ON EGO!
- *PLEASE STOP SEEKING THE 'NEXT BEST THING' AND LEAVE IT TO THE DETECTIVES.
- AT SOME POINT, YOU WILL REALISE THAT DESIRES LEAVE YOU EMPTY, ALONE AND UNHAPPY. BALANCE IS KEY.
- ONLY YOU DECIDE YOUR PATH, YOU CAN CONTINUE ON THIS JOURNEY OF 'DESIRE' BUT ONE DAY (I SUGGEST SOONER) YOU MUST OR YOUR LACK OF HEALTH AND BALANCE WILL STOP YOU...TO REMIND YOU THE IMPORTANCE IN APPRECIATING THE SIMPLICITY IN LIVING FOR NOW, ENJOYING EACH DAY, WITH THE SPECIAL PEOPLE IN YOUR LIFE.
- REMEMBER, YOU ARE LUCKY FOR ALL YOU HAVE.

FOR NOW:
- DESIRE TO LIVE EACH DAY WITH HAPPINESS.
- DESIRE WHAT YOU HAVE, NOT WHAT YOU THINK YOU NEED IN A MOMENT OF PLEASURE.
- PLEASE STOP HIDING BEHIND ANY MASK OF 'DESIRE'
- FIGHT YOUR FEARS... YOU ARE STRONG ENOUGH.
- BE HAPPY IN YOU, IN YOUR LIFE, HERE AND NOW.

RESULT: YOU WILL CREATE MAGIC IN EACH MOMENT. THEN YOU WILL SEE YOUR TRUE DESIRES WILL COME TO LIFE!

"Tanha, desire in Pali, means thirst. And thirst can never be permanently satisfied. Acting on your desire leads to habitual ways of behaving, to automatic responses. You become entrapped in pursuing what you crave and miss out on what's genuinely important-awakening to the true nature of things."
Joan Duncan Oliver

DESIGN

Each day, naturally I embrace and work on my designing and creativity, as it is my passion. I see inspiration for design all around and so remain focused but open-minded allowing each project I work on to evolve in the moment.

Of course, I truly embrace all kinds of design industries as they are based around life, connecting people, creativity and balance. With designers singularly, I have so much respect for them, especially those who don't conform to an idea or trend. I follow the creators.

I have such a high regard for the industries of Art, fashion, interior, architecture and of course lighting. Especially in fashion, hair and make up, the seasons are transient and the industry moves so fast that to keep the balance between creativity and results are difficult.

Art, Architecture, interiors and lighting may move at a slower pace to fashion, but there remains this constant conflict between creativity and reaching figures. The ones who find this balance are the ones we see in the stores worldwide…

ARTISTS AND DESIGNERS SHOULD BE CHERISHED, AS THEY BRING LIFE TO ART AND ART TO LIFE!
Natasha RD

NOTE:
Art is nothing without practice and passion and moving this into action.
Everyone has creative ability.
Creating is in each day focusing on the positives.
In all situations, accepting a new way to live in balance.
Life is creativity-it so much more than just painting ☺
Even in Painting, it is a process.
Equally, Creativity is a process.
Apply Creativity to your life.
BE CREATIVE TODAY AND EACH DAY! N.R.D.

DESIGN- Art and Architecture:

ART AND ARCHITECTURE IS BEYOND THE
REALMS OF STRUCTURE AND ANALYSIS.
MY ART, DESIGNS AND LIGHTING ARE THERE
TO CREATE AND RE-CREATE:
A NEW SPACE.
A NEW IDEA.
A NEW WAY TO LIVE.
A NEW WAY TO THINK.
A NEW WAY TO EXPERIENCE.
REACHING ALL OF YOUR SENSES.
CREATING A SPACE TO ENJOY EACH MOMENT.
NATASHA ROCCA DEVINE

"I WISH TO CREATE SPACES WHERE
ALL OF YOUR SENSES ARE TOUCHED."

NRD

"A great architect is not made by way of a brain nearly so much as he is made by way of a cultivated, enriched heart." Frank Lloyd Wright

"Architecture is really about well-being. I think that people want to feel good in a space... On the one hand it's about shelter, but it's also about pleasure." **Zaha Hadid**

"Art is a lie that makes us realize truth." Pablo Picasso

DESIGN-Fashion:

"It is a time to look toward the future... Without denying the past."
MIUCCIA PRADA

"...VOGUE." MADONNA

"I love fashion, ... What I love is the ability to express yourself, to be able to make a product and shoot an ad campaign that tosses you out into the world and lets you have a voice in contemporary culture, iconography. Tom Ford

"Fashion is not something that exists in dresses only. Fashion is in the sky, in the street. Fashion has to do with ideas, the way we live, what is happening." Coco Chanel

DESIGN-HAIR, NAILS AND MAKE UP:

HAIR, NAILS AND MAKE UP ARE EXTENSIONS OF ART ON THE CANVAS (MODELS). THEY ARE ANOTHER PIECE OF THE PUZZLE IN COMPLETING THE FINISHED PIECE=ART IN FASHION.

"There are make up artists and there are make up appliers. For me it is an art." Ashely Shakespeare, Make up Artist, Boston

"Hair style is the final tip-off whether or not a woman really knows herself." Hubert de Givenchy, Vogue, July 1985

DETERMINATION

"Everything positive is achieved based on determination, but only without force and having good intentions from within." Nrd.

DREAM(S)

EVERYONE HAS DREAMS.
YOU MAY NOT REALISE BUT DREAMS REPRESENT A FANTASY OF YOUR
INNER VALUES THAT YOU WISH TO CREATE IN LIFE.

ACCORDING TO SIGMUND FREUD, DREAMS ALSO ARE AN IDEA OF
WHERE YOUR MIND IS AT ON A DAY TO DAY.
HE INTERPRETS DREAMS ON A DEEPER LEVEL.
IF YOU HAVE RE-OCCURING ONES, PLEASE TAKE NOTICE.
WRITE IT DOWN TO SEE WHY YOU MAY BE DREAMING LIKE THIS?
THEN WORK IT OUT AND LET IT GO…

IN LIFE, DREAMS SHOULD BE HONOURED AND
RESPECTED.
NEVER LET ANYONE TELL YOU THAT YOU
CAN'T DREAM.
KEEP DREAMING-NEVER STOP DREAMING.
DREAM BIG…EVERYTHING STEMS FROM THIS.

NOW, PUT THEM INTO ACTION.
START CREATING YOUR DREAMS TODAY! nrd

"EVERY HEAD WOULD BE HELD UP HIGH…
THERE'D BE SUNSHINE IN EVERYONE'S SKY,
IF THE DAY EVERY DAWNED…
WHERE I RULED THE WORLD." JAMIE CULLUM

**"I have spread my dreams beneath your feet.
Tread softly because you tread on my dreams.**"
W.B. Yeats

"Some men see things as they are
and ask "Why?"
I dream of things that never were
and say, "Why not?"
George Bernard Shaw

"THE MORE YOU THINK YOU KNOW WHAT'S RIGHT,
THE LESS YOU DO WHAT YOU FEEL INSIDE.
SO, I WON'T PRETEND THAT I ALWAYS KNOW,
I JUST FOLLOW MY HEART WHEREVER IT GOES.
AND I MAY NOT GET IT RIGHT,
BUT AT LEAST I'M LIVING, COZ I'VE ONLY GOT
THIS... ONE LIFE, ONE LIFE,
ONE LIFE AND I'M GONNA LIVE IT RIGHT."
JAMES MORRISON

EDUCATION:

I see education in terms of the sharing of Awareness of the teachers to the students in question. The teachers' or educators role in the education of children is integral and honorable in shaping their mindset and lives.

In terms of education in life, I believe in embracing each moment and taking in what is relevant. It is more than getting 'A's, repeating out a textbook or copying a design or method. It is about creating new ideas in each moment... that is education, which will last a lifetime.

"GUIDANCE IS NECESSARY. YET, I LEARN ALL THE RULES SO THEN I CAN BREAK THEM AND CREATE A NEW WAY." NRD

"Education is an admirable thing, but it is well to remember from time to time that nothing that is worth knowing can be taught." Oscar Wilde

EGO

EGO IS YOUR WORST ENEMY.

EGO CAUSES STRESS ON YOU and OTHERS IN YOUR LIFE.
EGO BLOCKS INTIMACY.
EGO BLOCKS CREATIVITY.
EGO BLOCKS FREEDOM AND FUN.

*LET GO OF YOUR EGO:
ALWAYS HAVE THE ABLITY TO LAUGH AT YOURSELF AND AT LIFE.
WITH AWARENESS OF YOURSELF AND OTHERS, THERE IS NO ROOM FOR EGO.
NO EGO=KEY TO HAPPINESS. NRD

"If you're too big to follow rivers, How you ever gonna find the sea? Emeli Sandé

EMOTIONAL FREEDOM TECHNIQUE (EFT)

According to Treacy O 'Connor, EFT practitioner, "Understanding that everything is made of degrees of vibrating energy, including ourselves, Emotional Freedom Technique, allows us to tap into the energy field of our physical body and release negative energy that may cause trauma, addiction, anxiety or physical injury.

EFT is accessible to everyone and is an easy method of healing based on the principles of Acupuncture, but using a tapping motion with our fingertips on various major meridian points. When we use EFT to clear issues, it raises our vibration to the highest possible level for us at that moment in time, hence bringing renewed awareness on a continuous basis."

ENCOURAGEMENT

"We all need encouragement in life. The tough love, negative approach to working, teaching or living does not bode well with me. It is based on a hierarchy system of egos and control.

We don't need to hold hands and sing together each day, but a little encouragement is best. It leads to excitement and positivity. This inevitably leads to creation and better results. This is a simple solution to success in work, school and life." Natasha Rocca Devine

"Nine tenths of education is encouragement."
Anatole France

ENVISION

YOU CAN ENVISION THE LIFE YOU WISH FOR.

NOW, YOU MUST CREATE THIS LIFE!

IT IS UP YOU... START NOW.

BE THE PERSON YOU DESERVE TO BE.

ENERGY

PLEASE take RESPONSIBILITY for the energy that YOU BRING into our space.

ENERGY HEALING

I had some energy sessions with Alla Svirinskaya, which I found very powerful. She explained to me of the power of the energy within yourself. Also, how the balance (or imbalance) in your energy (feminine in my case) effects your interactions and how your energy field attracts others in your life. It is so powerful.

From her book, especially from an interior architecture perspective, her concepts of energy of the home and clearing this made huge sense. I see design beyond the realms of the structure and this reminded me of the importance of clearing energy, when moving in or designing new spaces in old structures.

Her meditation retreat cd allows you to relax, re-centre yourself and return to balance... and back into the moment.

BALANCED ENERGY IS KEY TO HAPPINESS. NRD.

"I learned that each organ has its own energy field and frequency, as does each illness".

According to Alla, a person's aura has seven layers, three of which represent your physical, emotional and mental energy.

Alla's bio-energy balancing is about harmonizing people on these three important levels." Alla Svirinskaya

"Energy and persistence conquer all things."
Benjamin Franklin

EMBRACE

"In many cultures, including the Dagara, the idea is you sculpt your face as you live and each wrinkle shows a particular joy or pain you survived. You would never have a facelift to look younger or color your hair when it turns gray. That would be a loss of beauty, a loss of grace." Sobonfu E. Somé

"The ability to change, to adapt and adjust according to the ever-changing moment is the art of being alive. Health of mind and body is the natural outcome of this ability."
Robert St. John, Metamorphosis

EMPATHY

EMPATHY IS UNDERSTANDING OR TRYING TO UNDERSTAND OTHERS. NOT PITYING. TRY TO RELATE. NRD.

"Empathy is putting yourself in another's shoes to find out what exactly that person is feeling or going through at the given time. It basically refers to being at a common wavelength with someone."
Deepa Kodikal

"Leadership is about empathy. It is about having the ability to relate to and connect with people for the purpose of inspiring and empowering their lives." Oprah Winfrey

"I think empathy is a beautiful thing. I think that's the power of film though. We have one of the most powerful, one of the greatest communicative tools known to man."
Michelle Rodriguez

"True contentment comes with empathy." Tim Finn

"I've thought a lot about the power of empathy.
In my work, it's the current that connects me and my actual pulse to a fictional character, it allows me to feel, pretend feelings and sorrows and imagined pain."
Meryl Streep

FAITH

"TAKE THE FIRST STEP IN FAITH. YOU DON'T HAVE TO SEE THE WHOLE STAIRCASE, JUST TAKE THE FIRST STEP."

MARTIN LUTHER KING, JR.

ALWAYS HAVE FAITH.
YOU ARE THE DRIVER AND FAITH IS YOUR FUEL.
WITHOUT FAITH YOU WILL REMAIN AT THE STATION.
FAITH IS ESSENTIAL IN LIFE. NRD

"I AM YOU AND YOU ARE ME...
If YOU WANT IT, YOU'VE GOT TO BELIEVE...
BELIEVE IN YOURSELF...
COZ BEING FREE IS A STATE OF MIND.
IT'S ALL JUST A GAME....
WE ALL JUST WANT TO BE LOVED." LENNY KRAVITZ

FAME-FAÇADE…

Each person has many talents. So, sharing and being recognised for your talents is wonderful and important but only by the right people. Of course, some people's talents are seen on a grander scale but each person has a light to share with the world... Yet, be happy as you are and allow your talents to shine naturally. Having personal awareness of 'fame', it scares me how many people wish to enter into the new phenomenon of 'being famous' for the sake of fame and instant recognition. Especially young children.. Without realising, Fame is like a marriage… Most enter in with no awareness that it is a lifetime commitment with no control over which route it takes. For the lucky ones who are known for their talents e.g. acting, sports, architecture... they remain focused on these and accept this comes as part of their journey. For the ones searching for fame, it's a life of fighting egos and chaos is inevitable ...

Ask yourself why you wish to be famous? Also, why would you wish your partner or child to be famous? Do you wish to lose your privacy or them to lose theirs? For your child, to lose their one chance at having childhood innocence? Add constant scrutiny to yours/their life? It is for money? Trust me, there are simpler ways to make money... Power? Power is ego based.

FAME DOES NOT EQUATE HAPPINESS,SUCCESS ETC.
SUCCESS=BEING YOU=BEING BALANCED=HAPPY☺NRD

FAMILY

"My family are my biggest gift."

"When you look at your life, the greatest happiness's are family happiness." Joyce Brothers

"Our most basic instinct is not for survival but for family. Most of us would give our own life for the survival of a family member, yet we lead our daily life too often as if we take our family for granted." Paul Pearshall

FEARLESSNESS

IF YOU CLEAR YOUR BLOCKS, YOU WILL ELIMINATE YOUR FEARS ON A FUNDAMENTAL LEVEL.
FEAR WILL BE SOMETHING YOU WILL ACCEPT AND OVERCOME.
WITHOUT FEAR, YOU WILL COME TO LIFE IN EVERY MOMENT.

"Start by doing what's necessary, then what's possible and suddenly you are doing the impossible." Francis of Assisi

"How you get so fly? From not being afraid to fall out the sky." Jay Z

FEELINGS

FEEL YOUR FEELINGS.
BLOCKING THEM WILL ONLY DELAY THE INEVITABLE.
FEEL, LET GO AND BE HERE NOW.

"Being must be felt.
 It can't be thought." Eckhart Tolle

FEMININITY

Embrace other women. It is not about comparison to others and competition. This behavior should be left for the sports field.
Each woman is beautiful, unique and deserves to be happy. NRD.

TASK: Focus on **your own** strengths.
Cherish your **female friends**.
Cherish women.
Compliment women.
STOP THE NEGATIVITY.
START TO CREATE POSITIVITY
AMONGST WOMEN...
Remember we are all on the same journey, but just on different paths.

"AND ALL MY SISTERS COMIN TOGETHER,
SAY YES I WILL,
YES I CAN,
COZ I AM A SUPERWOMAN,
YES, I CAN, YES, I WILL..." ALICIA KEYS

*LADIES, FEMININITY IS OUR
STRENGTH! EVEN IN HEELS
(OPTIONAL) OR WITH SENSITIVITY,
YOU'RE STILL A STRONG WOMAN...
ALWAYS HONOUR YOUR FEMININITY!

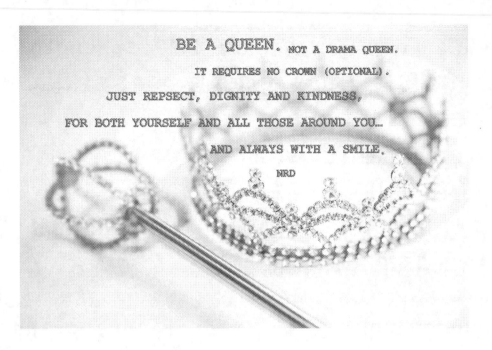

BE A QUEEN. NOT A DRAMA QUEEN.

IT REQUIRES NO CROWN (OPTIONAL).

JUST REPSECT, DIGNITY AND KINDNESS,

FOR BOTH YOURSELF AND ALL THOSE AROUND YOU...

AND ALWAYS WITH A SMILE.

NRD

FOOD

"This is my invariable advice to people: Learn how to cook- try new recipes, learn from your mistakes, be fearless, and above all have fun!" Julia Child, My Life in France

*REPLACE THE WORD "ADDICTED" TO CHOCOLATE, COFFEE ETC. FOR "AMORE" OR "LOVE" INSTEAD... BALANCE IS KEY SO STOP DEPRIVING YOURSELF.

LIFE'S TOO SHORT TO BE SO HARD ON YOURSELF. * STOP ANALYSING IT. IF YOU WANT IT- EAT IT. ENJOY IT... ENJOY FOOD. ENJOY LIFE. ENJOY NOW. ☺ NRD.

FOOD CONNECTS CULTURES.

FOOD CONNECTS PEOPLE HERE AND NOW.

PAST TO PRESENT=FOOD LOVE FOOD... LOVE NOW. NRD.

TRY IT: YOU DON'T NEED TO TRAVEL TO TRY A NEW FOOD. AT HOME, TRY A NATIONAL FOOD FROM SOMEWHERE ELSE AROUND THE WORLD.
HERE ARE SOME IDEAS:

- **Afghanistan:** Kabuli Pulao (baked rice, lentils, raisins, carrots and lamb)
- **Albania:** Tavë Kosi (Lamb and yogurt), Byrek shqiptar me perime (vegetable pies), Mish Qingjji me Barbunja (veal with lime beans)
- **Algeria:** couscous, Mechoui (lamb on a spit)
- **Andorra:** Trinxat (fried pancake with meat and vegetables)
- **Angola:** Prawns on skewer, Swordfish kebabs
- **Antigua and Barbuda:** Fungee (bread patty similar to polenta but made of corn meal). Pepperport (meat and spinach stew)

- **Argentina**: Churrasco con Chimichurri, Steak
- **Armenia**: basturma and sujukh (spicey beef), mushroom julienne, mountain yogurt (matsun, mah-TSOON)
- **Australia**: Vegemite
- **Brazil**: Feijoada
- **Canada**: Maple syrup,
- Central African Republic
- **China**: Peking Duck
- **Egypt**: Ful Medames
- **El Salvador**: Nasi Goreng
- **Ethiopia**: Doro Wett
- **France**: Bouillabaisse, Macaroons, Leg of beef, roast kidneys or grilled rabbit
- **Germany**: Hamburger, Currywurst (sausage)
- **Greece**: Lamb and Eggplant Moussaka, Moussaka. Aubergine
- **Hong Kong**: Shrimp dumpling, Dim Sum
- **India**: Masala dosa, Lamb Khorma, Vegetarian Indian
- Sagar Ratna, Kebabs
- **Indonesia**: Nasi Goreng
- **Ireland**: Stew, Potatoes, Colcannon, beef, Oysters, Fish and chips
- **Italy**: Parma ham, Fettucini, Neapolitan Pizza, Pasta, Zabaglione, Bolognese, Gnocchi
- **Jamaica**: Jerk Chicken
- **Japan**: Tempura Shrimp and Vegetables, Sushi, Ramen (soup with meat)
- **Korea**: Galbi, Pork Adobo, Bibimbap,
- **Lebanon**: Falafel, Humous
- **Malaysia**: Nasi Lemak
- **Mexico**: Fajitas, Red Snapper Veracruzana, Tacos
- **Peru**: Ceviche (fish)
- **Philippines**: Lechon, Lumpia, Pork Adobo, bulalo (beef stew), banana heart salad, adobo (marinaded meat), bake
- **Poland**: Pierogies, Bigos
- **Singapore**: Roti prata, Laksa
- **South Africa**: Nasi Goreng
- **Spain**: Seafood paella, Tapas, Spanish Omlette
- **Sudi Arabia**: Kabsa

- **Thailand:** Moo nam tok, Tom Yum
- **Ukraine:** Borscht
- **United Kingdom:** Steak and Kidney Pie and Fish and Chips
- **United States of America:** Warm brownie and vanilla ice cream, Potato chips, Fried chicken, Texas Chili con Carne, milkshake.

FORGIVENESS

Everyone makes mistakes. It is part of growth. Yet, forgiveness must start within. Forgive yourself and others, learn and let go. Don't let your mistakes or someone else's in your past hold you back from being happy in this moment. It is your decision.

TASK: Make a list of situations where you or others made a mistake, which impacted your life. Now, write beside these a new list what you can learn from this?
*NOW, YOU HAVE THE OPPORTUNITY TO LET GO…
ACCEPT. SMILE. LEARN. LIVE FOR NOW.

"The practice of forgiveness is our most important contribution to the healing of the world."
Marianne Williamson

"Ask God for forgiveness, and leave your regrets in the past!" Rhianna

FREEDOM

I believe freedom is a state of mind. To be free is being
free within yourself. To know your truth and purpose and
to live freely in each day is the essence of freedom.

FREEDOM IS NOT RUNNING FROM LIFE, IT IS EMRACING EACH MOMENT FROM WITHIN.

Natasha Rocca Devine

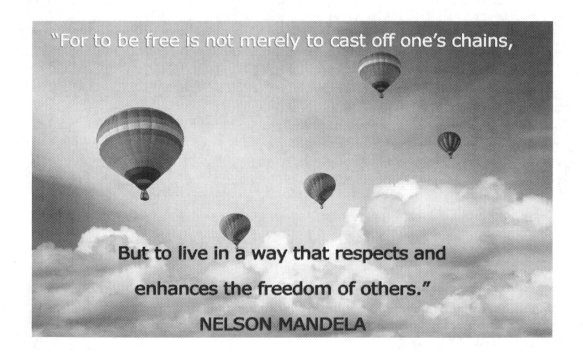

"For to be free is not merely to cast off one's chains,

But to live in a way that respects and

enhances the freedom of others."

NELSON MANDELA

FRIENDS

Friends to me are an extension of my family. I feel so fortunate for each one of my friends, individually and united: they add light to my life, as friends should. FRIENDSHIPS ARE INTEGRAL RELATIONSHIPS IN YOUR LIFE AND IN TERMS OF YOUR BALANCE SHOULD MATCH THIS!
*THE PEOPLE IN YOUR LIFE ARE A REFLECTION OF HOW YOU FEEL ABOUT YOURSELF, FRIENDS INCLUSIVE.
*YOU ARE WONDERFUL.
*YOU DESERVE WONDERFUL FRIENDS!
REMEMBER: FRIENDS SHOULD ADD TO YOUR LIFE!!!

"A faithful friend is the medicine of life."
The Apocrypha, 6:16

"I don't know what I'd do without my friends. I feel like I almost live my life to be able to have the luxury of being around them. And I feel like, if I've got in touch with what is important in life, my friends are the first thing on my list. They are my heart." Drew Barrymore

"Friends, they cherish ones another's hopes. They are kind to another's dreams." Henry David Thoreau

GENEROSITY

"Are you prepared to give that which you wish to receive?" Gordon Livingstone

GENERALISATIONS:

◊ FOR EXAMPLE: 'NORMAL': THIS IS AN ABSTRACT CONCEPT AS ONLY YOU DEFINE 'YOUR IDEA OF 'NORMAL''.

◊ E.G. 'BIG', 'SMALL', 'TALL', 'SLIM', 'HAPPY', 'SAD', 'SUCCESSFUL', 'RICH'... THESE CONCEPTS ARE ALL OBJECTIVE AND PENDING ON YOUR IDEAS

◊ E.G. 'RICH'= HAPPINESS V. INCOME?

◊ TO SOMEONE ELSE IT WILL MEAN SOMETHING ELSE..

◊ SO, IN LIFE PLEASE STOP GENERALISING AND LABELLING!

◊ SEASONS CHANGE.

◊ THINGS CHANGE.

◊ PEOPLE CHANGE.

◊ LIFE CHANGES.

◊ TASK: ALLOW YOURSELF AND OTHERS FREEDOM TO LIVE AND THINK OUTSIDE THE BOXES THAT YOU ARE CONFINED TO.

◊ SET YOURSELF FREE FROM THESE LIMITS.

◊ LIFE IS ABOUT BEING OPEN TO ALL THE POSSIBLIITIES THAT COME YOUR WAY.

◊ LIVE IN THE MOMENT AND EMBRACE EACH DAY.

GOALS

A goal is a good focus; like working on a new project, booking into a course, taking a new gym class or saving for a holiday.
Yet, on the way you must be open to change.
*A goal can't be too rigid as it must be adapted to the present moment. Nrd

"Follow your passion. Stay true to yourself. Never follow someone else's path unless you're in the woods and you're lost and you see a path. By all means, you should follow that." Ellen DeGeneres

"You are never too old to set another goal or to dream a new dream."
C. S. Lewis

GOSSIP

STOP GOSSIPING!!!
OTHERS WILL ALWAYS LOOK BETTER OR
WORSE OFF BUT YOU HAVE NO IDEA WHAT IS
GOING ON IN THEIR LIVES. SO FORGET IT.

GOSSIP IS THE WORST TIME WASTER.
IT IS CHEAP.
IT IS NEGATIVE.

NEW OPTION: CHANNEL THAT ENERGY INTO
SOMETHING PRODUCTIVE. YOU WILL BE
SURPRISED HOW MUCH BETTER YOU FEEL.

GRATITUDE

"Gratitude unlocks the fullness of life. It
turns what we have into enough and more.
It turns denial into acceptance, chaos to
order, and confusion to clarity. It can turn
a meal into a feast, a house into a home, a
stranger into a friend. Gratitude makes
sense of our past, brings peace for today
and creates a vision for tomorrow." Melody
Beattie

GROWTH

- PLEASE ALLOW YOURSELF AND OTHERS THE FREEDOM TO GROW AND EVOLVE EACH DAY.
- TASK: NOTE WHAT YOU TALK ABOUT, THINK ABOUT, READ AND WATCH AND HOW IT GROWS IN YOUR LIFE; CONSCIOUSLY AND SUBCONSCIOUSLY. IT IS ENERGY…
- ENERGY CREATES ENERGY.
- REALISE THE POWER OF YOUR ACTIONS
- AND THOUGHTS IN EACH DAY.
- WASTE NO TIME TALKING, THINKING OR VIEWING NEGATIVE THINGS… DETACH!
- ONLY YOU DECIDE IN WHICH DIRECTION YOU TAKE AND GROW IN LIFE.

*CHOSE ONLY POSITIVE GROWTH!
NATASHA ROCCA DEVINE

"THERE IS NO LIMIT TO HOW HIGH WE CAN GO, IF WE DON'T LOOK DOWN…
LET'S GO HIGHER AND HIGHER."
Jennifer Hudson

"Some changes look negative on the surface but you will soon realize that space is being created in your life for something new to emerge." Eckhart Tolle

"The day came that the risk to remain tight in the bud was more painful..

Than the risk it took to blossom."

Anais Nin

Habits

THROUGH METAMORPHOSIS AND 'AWARENESS', I SEE
HABITS AS BLOCKS/PATTERNS THAT WE ALL HAVE.
IN ORDER TO LET GO WE MUST RELEASE BLOCKS-ON
A FUNDAMENTAL LEVEL, WHICH ALLOWS US TO LIVE
IN THE MOMENT AND IN BALANCE.
THERE ARE MANY WAYS TO DO SO…

TASK: PLEASE FIND YOUR WAY TO RID HABITS.
YET, REMEMBER IT IS A DAILY PROGRAMME!!!
Habits can be good or bad but it is
important to be open to change and let go of
patterns. This will allow you to live in the
moment and without constraint.
AIM=LIVE FOR NOW IN BALANCE=HAPPINESS.

A MOMENT OF TRUTH-DO YOUR HABITS:
HURT YOU?
HURT OTHERS?
JEOPARDISE YOUR HEALTH?
HURT YOUR RELATIONSHIPS?
AFFECT YOUR FINANCES?
AND HOLD YOU BACK IN YOUR LIFE?

- *IF SO, PLEASE FIND SOLUTIONS TO LET GO OF THESE HABITS.
- DON'T LET A HABIT WIN OVER YOU.
- YOU ARE STRONG ENOUGH.
- YOU ARE HUMAN-ACCEPT HABITS.
- EXPECT CHALLENGES BUT FIGHT ON.
- EVEN IF YOU LOSE TO A HABIT,
- GET BACK UP AND FIGHT AGAIN.
- YOU DECIDE THIS:
- DECIDE TO WIN. DECIDE TO HEAL.
- DECIDE BALANCE.
- DECIDE HAPPINESS. NRD

"THE DRUGS DON'T WORK THEY ONLY MAKE IT WORSE" THE VERVE

H20

H20=A HAPPY BODY AND MIND

HARMONY

"Peaceful in body, peaceful in speech, the bhikkhu who is peaceful and well-concentrated. And who has rejected the world's bait is called "one at peace." Dhammapada

YOUR HARMONY= HEALING AND FAITH=CREATIVITY=

BALANCE= HAPPINESS=HUMOUR=POSITIVE ENERGY=

HOPE=LIGHT= HARMONY IN THE WORLD. NRD

HAPPINESS

The concept of Happiness is a means of perspective but deep down we all know what will create happiness in our own life. It begins within…

IT IS UP TO YOU TO CREATE HAPPINESS FOR YOURSELF AND IN YOUR LIFE. REMEMBER, HAPPINESS IS A DECISION.

"Most folks are as happy as they make up their minds to be." Abraham Lincoln (1809-1865)

"We all live with the objective of being happy: our lives are all different and yet the same."

Anne Frank (1929-1945)

"Don't Seek Happiness. If you seek it, you won't find it, because seeking is the antithesis of happiness." Eckhart Tolle

HEALTH AND HEALING

BE HEALTHY: BODY AND MIND.
HEAL YOURSELF…
AND YOU'LL HEAL OTHERS WITH YOUR BALANCE.

HELP AND HELPING

Everyone has blocks to overcome. Asking or seeking help is a sign of strength and shows your humanity. The result should be HOPE AND OPTIONS FOR A POSITIVE CHANGE.

IF YOU ARE OFF BALANCE…
DON'T BE HARD ON YOURSELF.
ASK FOR HELP.
HELP YOURSELF.
HELP OTHERS.
YOU DESERVE HAPPINESS.
EVERYONE DESERVES HAPPINESS.

"When you're drowning, you don't say 'I would be incredibly pleased if someone would have the foresight to notice me drowning and come and help me,' You just scream." John Lennon

HERBAL MEDICINE

According to the National Herbalist Association of Australia, "herbal medicine is the oldest and most widely used system of medicine in the world today. It is medicine made exclusively from plants and is used in all societies and is common to all cultures."

HOME

"Home is not where you live but where they understand you." Christian Morganstern

"Everyday is a journey and the journey itself is home." Matsuo Basho

HOMEOPATHY

German Physician Dr. Samuel Hahnemann developed homeopathy when he noticed that the essence of the bark of the cinchona salisaya used to treat malaria, caused malaria symptoms when taken orally. According to the Society of Homeopaths, homeopathy treats the person with highly diluted non-toxic substances, mainly in pill form to trigger the body's natural system of healing.

"Only freedom from prejudice and tireless zeal avail for the most holy of the endeavors of mankind, the practice of the true art of healing." Samuel Hahnemann, Founder of Homeopathy

HOPE

"Hope is a thing with feathers
That perches in the soul:
And sings the tune without words
And never stops at all." Emily Dickinson

"Hope is a waking dream." Aristotle

HUGS

"Hugs can do great amounts of good, especially for children."
Princess Diana, Princess of Wales

HUMANITY

"Love and compassion are necessities, not luxuries. Without them humanity cannot survive."
Dalai Lama

HUMILITY

"It is amazing what you can accomplish if you do not care who gets the credit." Harry S. Truman

"There is no respect for others without humility in one's self."
Henri Frederic Amiel

HUMO(U)R

Humour to me is necessary for survival. It must begin with 'U'. I believe that there is always room for laughter. I am so fortunate to have a family and friends that have a wonderful sense of humour. I believe no matter what the situation, there is always room for a smile. It reminds us that there is hope.

"Humor is the affectionate communication of insight." Leo Rosten

"The secret to humor is surprise." Aristotle

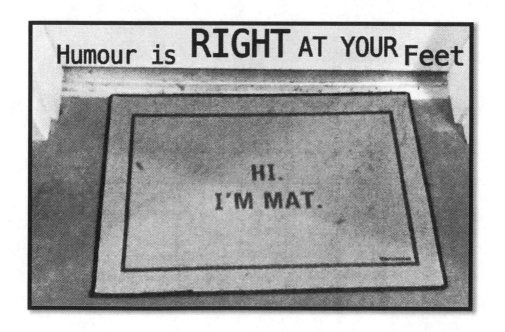

I AM

You are what you believe in this moment. NOT WHAT OTHERS ASSUME OF YOU. Allow yourself freedom to change and grow. You are not the person you were ten years ago, or even ten days ago. Be you today.

"I took a deep breath and listened to the old brag of my heart. I am, I am, I am."
Sylvia Plath

IDEAS

"The best way to have a good idea is to have a lot of ideas." Linus Pauling

IGNITE YOURSELF IN EVERY MOMENT

"Every mistake we made occurred because in moment we made it, we were not in conscious contact with our highest self. We were not centered in spirit. This is why making contact and spending time daily fostering it is most powerful thing we can do."
Marianne Williamson,

"Deep in my heart the answer it was in me, and I made up my mind to find my own destiny" Lauren Hill

IGNORANCE

Not knowing is acceptable.
JUDGING ON WHAT YOU DON'T KNOW IS IGNORANT. OPEN YOUR MIND. NRD

"Nothing in the world is more dangerous than sincere ignorance and conscientious stupidity." Martin Luther King, Jr.

"What you choose not to look at in your life rules your life." **Lynn Andreas**

IMAGINATION

"Imagination is more important than knowledge." Albert Einstein

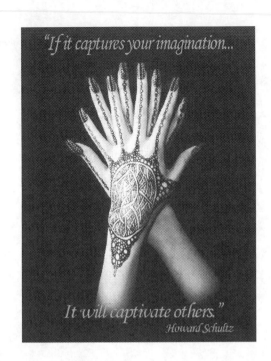

"If it captures your imagination...

It will captivate others."
Howard Schultz

NAIL ARTIST MEGUMI MIZUNO
http://www.facebook.com/megumi.mizuno

INCOME

Income is necessary for survival.
It is the exchange of energy to value your time invested in something you do. Those who create income through hard work and honesty have true wealth in life.
*THOSE WHO ARE PRACTICAL, BUT THEN SEE PAST THE EGO OF MONEY AND USE THAT INCOME EACH DAY TO PROTECT, PROVIDE AND ENJOY THIS INCOME WITH THEIR FAMILY AND FRIENDS…
THEIR INTEGRITY IS PRICELESS.
THEIR INCOME IS GOLD. NRD.

INNER JOY

"Is there a difference between happiness and inner peace? Yes. Happiness depends on conditions being perceived as positive: inner peace does not." Eckhart Tolle

INSIGHT

INSIGHT IS THE ABILITY TO SEE CLEARLY YOUR OWN TRUTH. NRD

"Insight enables you to know your own heart," Unknown.

INSPIRATION

Q and A:
WHO INSPIRES YOU?
WHY?
WHAT CAN YOU LEARN FROM THEM?
INSPIRE AND BE INSPIRED NOW...

"Just don't give up trying to do what you really want to do. Where there is love and inspiration, I don't think you can go wrong." Ella Fitzgerald

"Whenever there is inspiration...and enthusiasm...there is a creative empowerment that goes far beyond what a mere person is capable of." Eckhart Tolle

INTEGRITY

"More than any other trait, the presence of absence of honesty, that is integrity, is a window into the soul of another person."
Gordon Livingston

INTIMACY

Intimacy depends solely on each relationship. Yet, the core to this is being entirely yourself with the person or people in your lives. It may be 'cool' or 'typical' but I have zero tolerance for games in any relationships. It is your end goal to find happiness and intimacy so cut the childish games and be yourself from day one. The right person or friends will cherish you… but in order to meet them, first you must allow them meet the real you ☺

"True intimacy is standing emotionally naked in front of another person." Marianne Williamson

INTUITION

Intuition is part of living in the moment and making a decision based on your gut feeling at that time. When you are in balance, all of your actions will be based on your intuition in that moment. These will be the most creative. Honour this and be true to yourself in every moment.

"The Intuitive Mind is a sacred gift and the rational mind is a faithful servant. We have created a society that honors the servant and has forgotten the gift."
Albert Einstein

"You have to leave the city of your comfort and go into the wilderness of your Intuition. What you'll discover will be wonderful. What you'll discover is yourself." Alan Alda

"The intellect has little to do on the road to discovery. There comes a leap in consciousness, call it Intuition or what you will, the solution comes to you and you don't know how or why." **Albert Einstein**

"Follow your instincts. That's where true wisdom manifests itself." Oprah Winfrey

"When making a decision of minor importance, I have always found it advantageous to consider all the pros and cons. In vital matters, however, such as the choice of a mate or a profession, the decision should come from the unconscious, from somewhere within ourselves. In the important decisions of personal life, we should be governed, I think, by the deep inner needs of our nature." Sigmund Freud

Journey

EACH DAY CONTINUE ON YOUR JOURNEY.

NEVER FORGETTING WHERE YOU CAME FROM...

AND WHERE YOU WISH TO GO.

YET, ENJOYING TODAY. "VIVA PER ORA"...

NATASHA ROCCA DEVINE

"Often people attempt to live their lives backwards: they try to have more things, or more money, in order to do more of what they want so they will be happier. The way it actually works is the reverse.

You must first be who you really are, then, do what you need to do, in order to have what you want."
Margaret Young

KARMA

This is the natural law that suggests what you give out in life; you receive back in other ways. According to Buddha "We are all the product of our past, and past lives, but the future is not pre-determined. We have the choice-and responsibility-to make of life what we will."

You have a choice to live in good karma. BE POSITIVE.

KINDNESS

MY DAD ALWAYS TOLD ME 'CHARITY STARTS AT HOME' AND I BELIEVE THIS.
FIRST IT MUST BEGIN WITHIN, THEN WITH YOUR FAMILY AND FRIENDS... THEN YOU CAN REACH OUT.

YET, IF YOU ARE NOT KIND TO YOURSELF AND THE PEOPLE IN YOUR LIFE... THEN WHAT DOES IT MATTER THAT YOU ARE KIND TO OTHERS FAR AWAY?

TASK: EACH DAY BE KIND TO YOURSELF AND THOSE AROUND YOU, THEN AND ALWAYS DO REACH AFAR.
SEE HOW YOUR DAILY KINDNESS CAN IMPACT PEOPLE IN YOUR LIFE. NRD.

"Leave each person you meet a little better than you find them." Robin Sharma

KINESIOLOGY

According to the International College of Applied Kinesiology, "Applied Kinesiology (AK) evaluates structural, chemical and mental aspects of health using manual muscle testing with other standard methods of diagnosis." Other methods include joint mobilization, myofascial therapy, cranial techniques as well as meridian skills and holistic nutrition."

KISSES:

"BACI" (IN ITALIAN).
IN EACH CULTURE KISSING REPRESENTS INTIMACY..

- Whether it is kissing your family or friends on the cheek to greet them.

- It could be on your partner's forehead to show them respect.

- Perhaps kisses for your child each day, or if they have Fallen to show them you are healing this injury.

- Or best of all, if it is romantic on the lips to someone You love...

"And your heart's against my chest,
Your lips pressed in my neck.
I'm falling for your eyes,
But they don't know me yet.
And with a feeling I'll forget,
I'm in love now.
Kiss me like you wanna be loved
You wanna be loved, You wanna be loved.
This feels like falling in love…
We're falling in love." Ed Sheeran

INHALE LOVE.

EXHALE HATE. NRD

I say keep intimacy alive-keep kissing! (Strangers not included ☺☺) NRD

"You don't have to be cool to rule my world,
Ain't no particular sign I'm more compatible with...
I just want your extra time and your...
KISS!" PRINCE

"Come away with me,
 And we'll kiss on a mountaintop.
 Come away with me...
 And I'll never stop loving you." Norah Jones

LANGUAGES

Languages create connections. They can give you the option to travel, live and communicate to more people. It may not be a wish for you to learn another or more languages but it's always nice to know how to say 'hi and bye' when you visit a new place or meet someone from a different country. I have added a few here to start you off…

- Arabic - sabbah-el-khair (good morning), masaa-el-khair (good evening), Marhaba (Hello)

- Bahamas - hello (formal), hi or heyello (informal)

- Basque - kaixo (pronounced kai-show), egun on (morning; pronounced egg-un own), gau on (night; pronounced gow own)

- Bengali — namaskar

- Bulgarian - zdraveite, zdrasti (informal)

- Chinese - Cantonese nei ho (pronounced nay ho) Mandarin (pronounced ni hao)

- Croatian - boke (informal), dobro jutro (morning), dobar dan (day), dobra večer (evening), laku noć (night)

- Danish - hej (informal; pronounced hey), god dag (formal), god aften (evening; formal), hejsa (very informal).

- Dutch - hoi (very informal), hallo (informal), goedendag (formal)

- English - hello (formal), hi (informal)

- Finnish - hyvää päivää (formal), moi or hei (informal), moro (Tamperensis)

- **French** - salut (informal; silent 't'), bonjour (formal, for daytime use; 'n' as a nasal vowel), bonsoir (good evening; 'n' is a nasal vowel), bonne nuit (good night). There is also "ça va", but this is more often used to mean "how are you?"

- **Gaeilge (Irish)** - dia duit (informal; pronounced dee-ah gwitch; literally "God be with you")

- **German** - hallo (informal), Guten Tag (formal; pronounced gootan taag), Tag (very informal; pronounced taack).

- **Greek** - yia sou (pronounced yah-soo; informal), yia sas (formal)

- **Hawaiian** - aloha

- **Hebrew** - shalom (means "hello", "goodbye" and "peace"), hi (informal), ma kore? (very informal, literally means "whats happening" or "whats up")

- **Hindi** - namaste (pronounced na-mus-thei), kaise hain (a little formal), kaise ho (more informal, familiar)

- **Hungarian, Magyar** - jo napot (pronounced yoh naput; daytime; formal), szervusz (pronounced sairvoose; informal)

- **Icelandic** - góðan dag (formal; pronounced gothan dagg), hæ (informal)

- **Indonesian** - selamat pagi (morning), selamat siang (afternoon), selamat malam (evening)

- **Italian** - ciào (informal; also means "goodbye"), salve, buon giorno (morning; formal), buon pomeriggio (afternoon; formal), buona sera (evening; formal)

- **Japanese** - ohayou gozaimasu (pronounced o-ha-yo go-zai-mass), konnichi wa (pronounced ko-nee-chee-wa; daytime or afternoon), konban wa (pronounced gong-ban-wa; evening); moshi moshi (pronounced moh-shee moh-shee; when answering the phone); doumo (pronounced doh-moh; informal way of greeting,

- **Korean** - ahn nyeong ha se yo (formal; pronounced ahn-yan-ha-say-yo), ahn nyeong (informal; can also be used to mean "goodbye")

- **Kurdish** — choni, roj bahsh (day; pronounced rohzj bahsh)

- **Latvian** - labdien, sveiki, chau (informal; pronounced chow).

- **Lithuanian** - laba diena (formal), labas, sveikas (informal; when speaking to a male), sveika (informal; when speaking to a female)

- **Luxembourgish** - moïen (pronounced MOY-en)

- **Malayalam** - namaskkaram

- **Maltese** - merħba (meaning "welcome"), bonġu (morning), bonswa or il-lejl it-tajjeb (evening)

- **Maori** - kia ora

- **Mongolia** - sain baina uu? (pronounced saa-yen baya-nu; formal), sain uu? (pronounced say-noo; informal)

- **Nepali** - namaskar, namaste, k cha (informal), kasto cha

- **Norwegian** - hei ("hi"), hallo ("hello"), heisann ("hi there"), halloisen (very informal).

- **Persian** - salaam or do-rood (see note above - salaam is an abbreviation, the full version being as-salaam-o-aleykum in all Islamic societies)

- **Polish** - dzień dobry (formal), witaj (hello) cześć (hi)

- **Portuguese** - oi, boas, olá or alô (informal), bom dia (good morning), boa tarde (good afternoon), boa noite (good evening).

- **Romanian** - salut, buna dimineata (formal; morning) buna ziua (formal; daytime) buna searaformal; evening)

- **Russian** - pree-vyet (informal), zdravstvuyte (formal; pronounced ZDRA-stvooy-tyeh)

- **Senegal** - salamaleikum

- **Serbian** - zdravo (informal), dobro jutro (morning,

- **Slovak** - dobrý deň (formal), ahoj (pronounced ahoy), čau (pronounced chow) and dobrý (informal abbreviation)

- **Slovenian** – živjo (informal; pronounced zhivyo), dobro jutro (morning), dober dan (afternoon), dober večer (evening; pronounced doh-bear vetch-air)

- South African English - hoezit (pronounced howzit; informal)

- **Spanish** - holà (pronounced with a silent 'h': o-la), alo, que pasa (Spain, informal)

- **Swahili** - jambo

- Swedish - hej (informal; pronounced hey), god dag (formal)

- Tagalog (Pilipino - Philippines) - kumusta ka (means "how are you?")

- Thai - sawa dee-ka (said by a female), sawa dee-krap (said by a male)

- Tsonga (South Africa) - minjhani (when greeting adults), kunjhani (when greeting your peer group or your juniors)

- Turkish - merhaba (formal), naber? (Informal)

- Ukranian - dobriy ranuke (formal; morning), dobriy deyn (formal; afternoon), dobriy vechir (formal; evening), pryvit (informal)

- Urdu - adaab

- Vietnamese - xin chào

- Welsh - shwmai (North Wales; pronounced shoe-my)

- Zulu - sawubona

LAUGHTER

"YOU CAN TURN PAINFUL SITUATIONS AROUND THROUGH LAUGHTER. IF YOU CAN FIND HUMOR IN ANYTHING EVEN POVERTY, YOU CAN SURVIVE ANYTHING."

BILL COSBY

"Everybody laughs the same in every language because laughter is a universal connection." Yakov Smirnoff

LET GO…

PLEASE LET GO OF:
THOUGHTS
ANYTHING or ANYONE who holds you back on your path in life.
REMEMBER…
HAPPINESS AND BALANCE IN EACH DAY IS YOUR DESTINATION.
NATASHA ROCCA DEVINE

LIFE

"Life isn't about finding yourself.
Life is about creating yourself."
George Bernard Shaw

"To believe in something and not to live it is dishonest." Gandhi

"Life always whispers at first, if you ignore the whispers, life screams."
Oprah Winfrey

"Fear less, Hope more:
Eat less, Chew more:
Whine less, Breathe more:
Talk less, Say more:
Hate less, Love more:
and all good things are yours."
Swedish Proverb

"DON'T RAIN ON MY PARADE.
LIFE'S TOO SHORT TO WASTE ONE DAY...
I'M GONNA RISK IT ALL, THE FREEDOM TO FALL.
IT SURE LOOKS GOOD TO ME...
GIVE LOVE LIFE, GIVE LOVE..." ALICIA KEYS

LIGHT

IF YOU WISH TO DO SOMETHING POSITIVE FOR SOMEONE ELSE THEN SHARE LIGHT...

TASK: PLEASE LIGHT CANDLES FOR ANYONE YOU WISH TO SEND POSITIVE ENERGY TO. IT MAY BE SOMEONE WITH A SICKNESS, TO WISH THEM WELL DURING AN EXAM, INTERVIEW OR SOMEONE WHO IS ANGRY. PLEASE SEND THEM POSITIVE ENERGY...NRD

"Darkness cannot drive out darkness:
only light can do that.
Hate cannot drive out hate:
only love can do that."
Martin Luther King Jr., *A Testament of Hope: The Essential Writings and Speeches*

"There are two ways of spreading light: To be the candle, or the mirror that reflects it." Edith Wharton

"Everything is shown up by being exposed to light, and whatever is exposed to light itself becomes light." St. Paul.

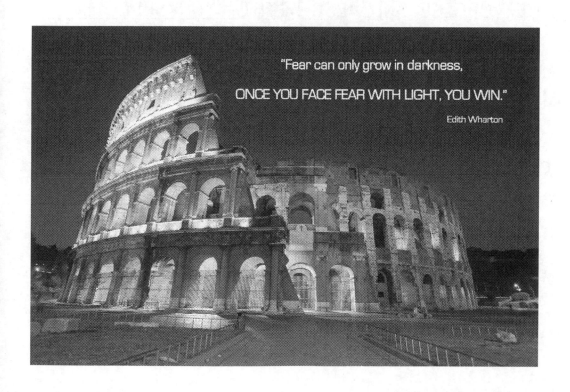

"Fear can only grow in darkness,
ONCE YOU FACE FEAR WITH LIGHT, YOU WIN."
Edith Wharton

LIGHT AND HEALING

As a lighting designer (and Metamorphosis practitioner), I have researched and experienced the implications of having light in your life. This is related to finding light in your daily life; home, office and spaces you are in. Also, linked to positivity and finding your light within.

Yet, having lived in London and other cities, I witness so many people moving from home to work, via tubes/trams/cars, to offices, to gyms/or straight home, with no natural light reaching them each day. It is inevitable that you will feel tired and off balance and look for other options to keep your energy levels up.

TASK: LET LIGHT INTO YOUR LIFE...

FIND WAYS TO CREATE MORE LIGHT INTO YOUR HOME, OFFICE AND ALSO WITHIN YOURSELF.

LISTEN

Allow space to listen to others and yourself. Nowadays, people spend all their time on computers, phones calling, mailing, texting and in constant interaction with others but never present in that moment.

*Be honest: Ask yourself when did you last have a conversation with someone with only you and the other person present?

TASK: START LISTENING MORE TODAY! NRD

"Since in order to speak, one must first listen, learn to speak by listening." Rumi

"(Listen to yourself) to your body, mind, who is in your life, the way you live… All the signs are there. YOU DECIDE YOUR BALANCE IN EACH DAY… TAKE RESPONSIBILITY NOW. NRD

LOSS

LOSS AND LETTING GO IS
INEVITABLE IN LIFE:
EMBRACE IT.
FEEL IT.
IT IS NEVER EASY.
BUT YOU CAN AND
YOU WILL OVERCOME IT.
WHEN YOU DO,
YOU WILL BE STRONGER.
YOU DESERVE TO BE HAPPY.
PLEASE LET GO… NRD

LOVE IS IN EVERYTHING.
LOVE IS EVERYWHERE.
LOVE IS LIGHT.
LOVE IS LIFE.
LOVE IS THE HOPE, EVEN ON A RAINY DAY.
LOVE IS SEEING A YOUNG CHILD SMILE.
LOVE IS IN YOUR PARTNERS EYES.
LOVE IS IN YOUR FRIENDS LAUGHTER.
LOVE IS IN YOUR FAMILY.

MOST IMPORTANTLY,
LOVE IS IN YOURSELF.
LET LOVE OUT AND YOU WILL GET LOVE IN. NRD

"Love is doing small things with great love." Mother Teresa

Being in love also shines a light on the other person but also on whom you are.
It is a time when you are most vulnerable…
It scares most people to face themselves.
FIGHT YOUR FEARS… FALL IN LOVE. NRD

"Love one another and help others to rise to the higher levels, simply by pouring out love. Love is infectious and the greatest healing energy." **Sai Baba**

"LOVE IS MEANT TO HEAL.

LOVE IS MEANT TO RENEW.

LOVE IS MEANT TO MAKE US FEEL SAFE.

LOVE IS MEANT TO INSPIRE US WITH POWER.

LOVE IS MEANT TO MAKE US CERTAIN, WITHOUT DOUBT.

LOVE IS MEANT TO BRING PEACE." DEEPAK CHOPRA

"BECAUSE LOVE AINT GONNA LET YOU DOWN NO MORE..." JAMIE CULLUM

"Say it's true,
there's nothing like me and you.
Not alone, tell me you feel it too...
And I would runaway I would runaway,
Yeah I would runaway,
I would runaway with you.
Cause I have fallen in love With you...
I'm never gonna stop falling in love,
with you." The Coors

"WE'VE GOT TO LET LOVE RULE..."
LENNY KRAVITZ

"On my love you can rely and
I'll stay with you.
Oh I'll stay with you
Through the ups and the downs.
Oh I'll stay with you
When no one else is around.
And when the dark clouds arrive
I will stay by your side.
I know we'll be alright
I will stay with you.' John Legend

Magnetic Healing

This Japanese healing system is based on the fact that all matter is made up of energy. Therefore, the electromagnetic fields created by strong magnets can be used to balance the energy of the diseased body.

"A negative magnetic field can function like an antibiotic to help destroy bacterial, fungal and viral infections by promoting oxygenation and lowering the body's acidity." William H. Philpott, M.D.

MANAGE-YOUR EXPECTATIONS

YOU CAN ONLY MANAGE YOUR OWN EXPECTATIONS.

EACH DAY WILL BE A BATTLEFIELD IF YOU EXPECT YOURSELF AND OTHERS TO MEET ALL OF YOUR EXPECTATIONS....

NOTE: YOU CANNOT PLAN HOW THINGS OR PEOPLE WILL REACT. PLEASE BE OPEN TO CHANGE. LIVE IN THE MOMENT AND IN BALANCE, THE REST WILL WORK OUT AS IT IS MEANT TO. NRD

MASSAGE

According to the University of Maryland Medical Centre: "The use of massage for healing purposes dates back 4,000 years in Chinese medical literature and continues to be an important part of Traditional Chinese Medicine (TCM). A contemporary form of massage, known as Swedish massage, was introduced to the United States in the 1850s. By the end of the 19th century, a significant number of American doctors were practicing this manual technique." The methods of massage have and continue to grow across the world.

Pending on your symptom, there are nearly 100 different massage and body work techniques. Each technique is uniquely designed to achieve a specific goal. The most common types practiced in the United States include: Craniosacral massage: Myofascial release, Reflexology, Rolfing, Shiatsu, Sports massage, Swedish massage to list a few.

MASCULINITY

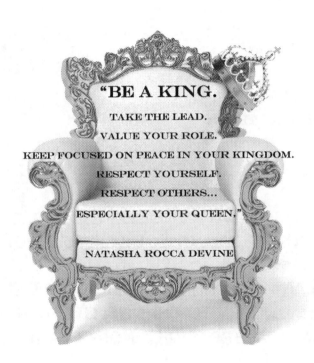

"BE A KING.

TAKE THE LEAD.

VALUE YOUR ROLE.

KEEP FOCUSED ON PEACE IN YOUR KINGDOM.

RESPECT YOURSELF.

RESPECT OTHERS...

ESPECIALLY YOUR QUEEN,"

NATASHA ROCCA DEVINE

It is clear, the masculine and feminine roles have shifted in recent years and caused so much confusion in terms of how men should act, especially towards women.
I believe CHIVALRY SHOULD AND MUST REMAIN.
Yet, we must allow men freedom to do so.
TODAY, it is time to STOP EMASCULATING MEN.

Negativity breeds negativity.
Positivity creates positivity.
HONOUR THE MEN IN YOUR LIFE. NRD

*NEW OPTION (FOR WOMEN):
Allow each man to be his own man.
To protect and provide.
To live life in balance.
Tell him what you need to be happy in love.
Ask him for his help, if you need help.
MEN LIKE TO FIND SOLUTIONS ☺
Remember that he is unique, as each man is.
Embrace his strengths.

Meanwhile, focus on your own balance and
this will create a better man in yours…
Just wait and see! Natasha RD

"It is not true that nice guys finish last.
Nice guys are winners before the game even
starts." Addison Walker

IT IS SUGGESTED THAT MEN APPRECIATE FACTS
AND VALUES. SO, OPINIONS TO A MAN ARE
SIMILAR TO FEELINGS TO A WOMAN.

SO, HIS OPINIONS ARE SEEN AS EXPRESSIONS OF HIMSELF. PLEASE RESPECT HIS OPINIONS: THEY ARE WHO HE IS. RESPECT HIM.
(This is why he WILL DEFEND these OPINIONS so much ☺) NATASHA RD

"Cause a real man, knows a real woman when he sees her,
And a real woman knows a real man ain't afraid to please her.
And a real woman knows a real man always comes first,
And a real man just can't deny a woman's worth." Alicia Keys

MEDITATION

Mediation is not limited to sitting and listening to calm music alone. This is a wonderful concept but for some, (especially those with young children and long hours in work) this may not be an option. There are always options…

For myself, meditation is (the concept of Metamorphosis): enjoying the moment and being fully present in now. For everyone, it can begin through many tasks such as; Running, painting, watching a movie, playing with your child, going on a hike… going to a football game.

TASK: Find your way to meditate!

METAMORPHOSIS:

Metamorphosis embodies the
concept of 'living in the moment'
by releasing blocks on a fundamental level,
beyond the symptom.

THE AIM IS TO CREATE A BALANCE
BETWEEN AFFERENCE AND EFFERENCE.
THIS IS A BALANCE BETWEEN THOUGHT
AND ACTION.
THIS IS LIVING IN EACH MOMENT.

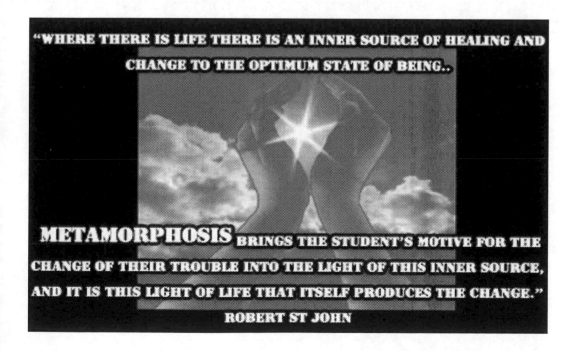

"WHERE THERE IS LIFE THERE IS AN INNER SOURCE OF HEALING AND CHANGE TO THE OPTIMUM STATE OF BEING..

METAMORPHOSIS BRINGS THE STUDENT'S MOTIVE FOR THE CHANGE OF THEIR TROUBLE INTO THE LIGHT OF THIS INNER SOURCE, AND IT IS THIS LIGHT OF LIFE THAT ITSELF PRODUCES THE CHANGE."

ROBERT ST JOHN

"Through the practice of Metamorphosis, you will move through your blocks: which are physical manifestations of unconscious patterns of stress from Post-Conception.
The blocks arise at various levels of consciousness.

These are the 7 levels of Consciousness:
1. Concept
2. Idea
3. Thought
4. Form
5. Creation
6. Action
7. Awareness

In Metamorphosis, we move through the levels of consciousness and into creation. If and when blocks arise (as illness) they are seen beyond the physical. It is a physical Manifestation of a deeper block in consciousness, which can be released through treatments.

Evidently, each individual has different blocks to overcome at different times, which are known as 'morphs'. They arise as in illness in the body. For instance around the stomach, which is the thought level, people on this block generally have digestive problems. Around the neck is the action level and so on.

Metamorphosis allows you to move through your blocks or 'morphs' and into creation on a fundamental level. Outside of treatments, there are hand symbols, which can be used to centre you into the moment on a day-to-day.

The practice of Metamorphosis is your own responsibility and you are self-healing without any dependency.
The practitioner is a catalyst.
Whilst practicing Metamorphosis, you are the healer.

Each time we release blocks we move further into creation in every moment. Living like this, there is no room for chaos, only creativity and light." NATASHA ROCCA DEVINE

TASK: PLEASE PRACTICE THE CREATION
BALANCE HAND SYMBOL (attached)
USE THIS SYMBOL THROUGHOUT YOUR DAY,
EXPERIENCE HOW THIS HAND SYMBOL WILL BRING
YOU INTO THE MOMENT.

THE AIM OF METAMORPHOSIS:
TO RELEASE BLOCKS.
TO FIND YOUR OWN BALANCE.
TO FIND YOUR OWN INNER AUTHORITY.
TO LIVE IN THE MOMENT,
EACH MOMENT.
EVERY MOMENT.
STARTING NOW!

MIND

"Life isn't as serious as the mind makes it out to be."

Eckhart Tolle

MOTIVATION

You must question your motivation in every action... WHAT ARE YOUR MOTIVATIONS IN YOUR RELATIONSHIPS, WORK IN AND LIFE?
*If your motivation is not from a place of creativity and balance then re-consider!

WHY CREATE CHAOS WHEN YOU CAN CREATE SOMETHING POSITIVE AND ORIGINAL?
WHY DON'T YOUR MOTIVATIONS FOCUS ON:
HAVING A GREAT RELATIONSHIP/PARTNER?
HAVING GREAT FRIENDSHIPS?
HAVING A JOB THAT HONOURS WHO YOU ARE?
AND LIVING A LIFE THAT ALLOWS YOU TO BE HAPPY? SECURE? BALANCED?

FACT: IT IS A SIMPLE EQUATION.
(*I KNOW THIS, AS MATHS IS NOT MY STRENGTH*)
 IT IS CALLED BALANCE.
TAKE THE LEAD. CUT THE CHAOS.

CREATIVITY IS THE NEW COOL NRD

MUSIC AND HEALING

I have awareness and sincere appreciation for musicians
and songwriters alike. With technological advancements:
IPods, YouTube etc. the industry has evolved at a rapid
pace. At any moment in time, music has the power to share
one person(S) experiences into creative songs with others
all around.
Each day, music continues to inspire me and assists me
with my Awareness of the world. I believe it helps
everyone to gain Awareness.
Music is AWARENESS=healing.

NOTE: PLEASE TAKE NOTE OF WHAT YOU LISTEN TO.
IT CAN AND WILL AFFECT YOUR MOOD. FOR EXAMPLE…
*IF YOU ARE FEELING UPSET, IT IS PROBABLY BEST NOT TO
LISTEN TO SAD SONGS…
IN THIS INSTANCE (AND IN GENERAL) PLEASE LISTEN TO UPBEAT,
POSITIVE MUSIC THAT WILL BRING YOU INTO THIS MOMENT ☺

"NO GURU, NO METHOD,
JUST YOU AND I AND NATURE."
VAN MORRISON.

"If you are gifted from God, He gives you the gift of the voice, and even the intelligence to drive it." Luciano Pavarotti

"I'm not really a songwriter-I'm an entrepreneur. So, in a sense I am an actress first and foremost. I act out the songs, and lead with my heart." Diana Ross

"How does one decipher between reality and make believe?
As I begin to whisper to myself the sounds I hear are not so much words, just sounds.
Light to the ear, soft on the tongue.
Sounds.
I hear the whimpering of a cry that should convey sadness, but in fact, depicts beauty.
Beauty of a sound not made by natural causes, oh no.
A sound that is displayed and sends ruptures of emotions through my skeletal system.
 A sound not only registers life, but also processed as a dream.
A descendent of notes on a chromatic scale.
A peace that cannot be imagined, it must be portrayed."
Chanel Valme, singer/songwriter, Boston and Miami

"I think music in itself is healing. It's an explosive expression of humanity. It's something we are all touched by. No matter what culture we're from, everyone loves music." Billy Joel

TASK: SING!!! GO TO A KARAOKE BAR...OR HAVE A KARAOKE NIGHT AT HOME WITH FRIENDS... SING WITH FRIENDS OR EVEN ALONE (NO ONE WILL KNOW). IT IS ALWAYS A WAY TO ENJOY A NIGHT OR EACH DAY TO GET YOU INTO THE MOMENT. NRD

Naturopathic Medicine

According to the American Association of Naturopathic Physicians, naturopathic medicine is "steeped in traditional healing methods, principles and practices. Naturopathic medicine focuses on holistic, proactive prevention and comprehensive diagnosis and treatment." Naturopaths use protocols that minimize harm, therefore facilitating the body's innate ability to restore and maintain health."

NATURE

TO DO: TAKE TIME OUT IN NATURE: WALKING, GARDENING, ENJOY THE VIEW. ENJOY THE MOMENT.

"Nature uses as little as possible of anything." Johannes Kepler, Astronomer

"What nature creates has eternity in it." Isaac Bashevis Singe

NEVER SAY NEVER…

NEVER LET ONE BAD EXPERIENCE OR RELATIONSHIP HOLD YOU BACK…YOU DON'T KNOW WHAT WAS GOING ON IN THE OTHER PERSON(S) LIFE. IT IS PART OF YOUR JOURNEY TO FIND THE ANSWER. THEN ACCEPT.

LET GO. BE HAPPY TODAY. NOW. NRD

NO

SAY NO When you wish IN LIFE.
IT IS IMPORTANT TO FIND YOUR OWN
BALANCE BETWEEN YES AND NO.
USE YOUR INSTINCTS IN THE MOMENT.
SAY YES ONLY IF YOU WISH. NRD

-NO REGRETS-
CHOICE: REGRET OR LET GO?
1. HOLD ON TO THE PAST AND RELIVE IT
OR
2. ACCEPT IT, LEARN FROM IT, MOVE ON AND
LIVE FOR NOW! NATASHA RD

NOW

"LIVE IN NOW.
NO NEED TO LOOK FOR EXCITEMENT...
JUST CHANGE YOUR OUTLOOK ON LIFE.
AS EACH DAY AND MOMENT IS EXCITING,
(Whether you do the same thing for one day or ten years),
As EVERY MOMENT happens
For the FIRST TIME,
For the ONLY TIME,
EVERY TIME." NRD

TASK: SURPRISE YOURSELF TODAY!

- DO SOMETHING DIFFERENT IN THE MOMENT.
- EVEN IF IT MEANS TAKING A NEW ROUTE
  TO WORK, TRYING A NEW FOOD,
  WEARING BRIGHTER COLOURS OR TAKING
  A CHANCE YOU WOULD NOT NORMALLY DO.
- BREAK THE OLD ROUTINE.
- LIVE FOR NOW-IT IS A LOT MORE FUN!

TRAVEL LIGHT. SHINE BRIGHT.

ACCEPT BUMPS ON YOUR WAY...

ENJOY EACH AND EVERYDAY. NRD

"AND MY MOMMA TOLD ME, THERE'LL BE DAYS LIKE THIS."
VAN MORRISON

NUTRITION

"In the pursuit of Excellence there are several areas of recognised importance, of which Nutrition is a vital cog in the wheel of balance.

The correct diet is of vital importance to all individuals, for the purpose of physical and emotional well being. Most common health problems can be prevented through a healthy diet.

The significance of nutrition to a healthy balanced life can never be underestimated."

John Devine

O₂

O2 IS NECESSARY FOR BALANCE EACH DAY…
PLEASE GET OUTSIDE FOR FRESH AIR!

OMEGA

According to Best Health Magazine, www.besthealthmag.ca/omega, Omegas are polyunsaturated fatty acids called "essential" fatty acids. Our body needs them but can't make them and thus they must come from our diet. Others include omega6 and Omega 9. Researchers believe our modern Western diet is unbalanced because it contains high amounts of omega6 fatty acids (from grains) and not enough omega3. Scientists believe omega-9, in fats such as olive oil, is neutral (it is not necessarily good for us yet is better to consume than unhealthy saturated fats). Most of us don't consume enough omega3. This imbalance may contribute to many health issues.

Omega-3 includes a range of fatty acids, including the 3 most important: eicosapentaenoic acid (EPA), docosahexaenoic acid (DHA), both found in oily fish and alpha-linoleic acid (ALA) from plants. These form part of the cell membrane of all cells and control what substances pass in and out of the cells and how they talk with one other. Cells with high levels of omega 3 in their membranes are more fluid and work more effectively.

ONE LIFE:

WE HAVE ONE LIFE…
STOP WAITING FOR IT TO START.
FIGHT YOUR FEARS.
WEAR THAT OUTFIT YOU'RE WAITING TO.
MAKE THAT CALL. GO ON THAT DATE.
TAKE THAT CHANCE. FALL IN LOVE.
START LIVING LIFE NOW. Nrd

"ONE LOVE.
ONE BLOOD.
ONE LIFE...
ONE LIFE,
WITH EACH OTHER."
BONO, U2.

ONWARDS...

'ONWARDS AND UPWARDS'-It is the best route to take in life!

STOP WAITING-YOU LEAD THE WAY...NRD

OPPORTUNITY

PLEASE CREATE YOUR OWN OPPORTUNITIES. THEY AWAIT YOU! NRD

"Opportunities multiply as they are seized."
Sun Tzu

"Healing is a matter of time, but it is sometimes also a matter of opportunity." Hippocrates

OPTIONS

There are always options in life. Although you may not see it at the time, you can always find options in every situation. It is about seeking the most creative ones for you. Anyone or anything that limits your options should be detached from your life-You are the leader in your life.

KEEP YOUR OPTIONS SIMPLE.
TOO MANY OPTIONS ARE WORSE THAN NONE.
YOU KNOW YOUR ONLY OPTION IS:
AN OPTION OF YOUR TRUTH. N.R.D.

OSTEOPATHIC MEDICINE

According to the American Association of Colleges of Osteopathic Medicine, "osteopathic medicine is a distinct form of medical practice in the United States. It provides modern medicine including prescription drugs, surgery, and technology to diagnose disease and evaluate injury by emphasizing health promotion and disease prevention."

Osteopathic doctors (OD), view the patient holistically, integrating physical, psychological and social needs. DOs learn that structure influences function. Therefore, if there is a problem in one area of the body's structure, function in that and other areas may be affected.

P<small>AIN</small>

Pain is part of your journey.
Yet, it is your awareness of this and ability to detach from previous pain from the past that counts.
TASK: Acknowledge pain in the moment and allow yourself to feel the feelings. Yet, accept that only you will suffer if you hold on to this pain. Let it out.
FIND YOUR WAY(S) TO LET GO.
BUT PLEASE LET IT GO. LIVE FOR TODAY.

TRUTH: NEVER EVER ACCEPT PHYSICAL, MENTAL OR EMOTIONAL ABUSE OFF ANYONE, WHICH CAUSES YOU PAIN.
SPEAK UP. SHOUT IF YOU NEED TO…
LET THEM AND OTHERS KNOW HOW YOU FEEL.
YOU DO NOT DESERVE PAIN!
YOU CONTROL THIS. NOT THEM.
FREE YOURSELF OF PAIN.
ALSO, LET GO OF PAIN WITHIN…
YOU ARE WORTHY OF HAPPINESS. nrd

"Pain is temporary. If I quit, however, it lasts forever."
Lance Armstrong

"Numbing the pain for a while will make it worse when you finally feel it."
J.K. Rowling, Harry Potter Author

"Turn your wounds into wisdom."
Oprah Winfey

"How can they deal with love if they're afraid to feel? Pain is meant to wake us up. People try to hide their pain. But they're wrong. Pain is something to carry, like a radio. You feel your strength in the experience of pain. It's all in how you carry it. That's what matters."
Jim Morrison

"Behind every beautiful thing, there's some kind of pain."
Bob Dylan

PARTY

EACH DAY IS A CELEBRATION.

PARTY TODAY. NRD.

PASSION(S)

PASSION IS MY MOTIVATION IN EACH DAY.
EVERYONE HAS PASSION(S): WHETHER IT IS FOR LIFE, PASSION
FOR PEOPLE AND/OR PASSION IN EACH DAY ALIKE.
TASK: FIND AND EMBRACE YOUR PASSION(S)!

"Your true passion should feel like breathing: it's that natural." Oprah Winfrey

"Nothing great was ever achieved without enthusiasm." Ralph Waldo Emerson

"Enthusiasm is everything. It must be taught and vibrating like a guitar string." **Pele**

PAST

"We all have a past, some run from it, block it, or hide it. Others live in their childhood as adults. Learn, from the bad memories, cherish the good ones and smile.
Today is the only moment you really have.
SO, PLEASE LIVE IT AND BE YOU TODAY." Natasha Rocca Devine

PATIENCE

Patience is allowing yourself to live for now and cherish the moment. It requires in believing that no matter happens in life, you are strong enough to cope and you are always in the right place now. Also, that if you are true to yourself, you will end up where you are meant to in each moment.

"Patience is the companion of wisdom." Saint Augustine

PERCEPTION

BE OPEN TO PERCEIVE A NEW EXPERIENCE IN EVERY MOMENT.

TO DO: TAKE A SERIOUS LOOK AT WHAT YOU ARE LOOKING AT EACH DAY: TV, BOOKS, MAGAZINES ETC.
THEY REFLECT YOUR PERCEPTION OF THE WORLD.
ENSURE THAT THEY ARE POSITIVE AND CREATIVE, AS THIS WILL INFLUENCE YOUR DAILY LIFE.

BE OPEN TO PERCEIVE LIFE IN A NEW WAY. EACH DAY.

"When you change the way you look at something, the thing you look at changes in response." **Heisenberg principle in physics**

"The eyes see only what the mind is prepared to comprehend."
Henri Bergson

"PERFECTION = A MYTH" NRD

PERSPECTIVE

"The one who follows the crowd will usually get no further than the crowd. The one who walks alone, is likely to find himself in places no one has ever been." Albert Einstein

"My mother drew a distinction between achievement and success. She said that achievement is the knowledge you studied and worked hard and done the best that is within you.

Success is being praised by others. That is nice but not as important or satisfying. **Always aim for achievement and forget about success."** Helen Hayes

PHYSICAL EXERCISE:

PHYSICAL EXERCISE IS MY PASSION. MY DAILY ROUTINE, WHICH ASSISTS A HEALTHY BODY AND MIND AND SOMETHING I ENCOURAGE FOR ALL.

TASK: FIND EXERCISE THAT IS/ARE SUITED TO YOU. IT SHOULD BE A BALANCE BETWEEN MAINTAINING YOUR HEALTH BUT ALSO ENJOYMENT. NEVER FORCE YOURSELF TO TAKE EXERCISE THAT IS HARMFUL TO YOU JUST TO BE SLIM, MUSCULAR ETC. TO SUSTAIN, IT MUST ALWAYS BE BALANCED. THERE ARE SO MANY TYPES OF EXERCISE FOR EVERYONE… DANCE, SPORT… SO, FIND YOURS! NRD

"Those who think they have no time for bodily exercise will sooner or later have to find time for illness." Edward Stanley

"PHYSICAL EXERCISE IS THE KEY TO WELL BEING... BOTH PHYSICALLY AND MENTALLY."

JOHN DEVINE

The three main types of exercise are: flexibility or range of motion, strength or resistance and endurance training (aerobic-with oxygen) or (nonaerobic-without oxygen):

1. Flexibility exercises increase joint flexibility and include stretching, running, Tai chi, yoga and golf.

2. Strengthening exercises increase muscle function and include two types: Isometric and Isotonic.

With **isometric**, muscles contract but joints don't move. Exercises are done against an immovable surface, for example, pressing your palm against a wall.

In **isotonic** exercise, a body part is moved and the muscle shortens or lengthens. A classic example of isotonic exercise is lifting free weights.

3. Endurance exercise improves stamina and requires exerting oneself for long periods of time.

Examples of **Aerobic exercise** include: walking, dancing, swimming and bicycling. **Anaerobic exercise** includes: weight lifting, sprints (running, biking), jumping rope, hill climbing, interval training, isometrics, or rapid bursts of hard exercise. The above information was taken from www.trulyhuge.com/news/tips55a.htm.

PHOTOGRAPHY (AND FILM)

I adore photography and see film as capturing a sequence of still images, which are collated into one story. Whilst I was working on various shoots, I was always fascinated about the role of D.O.P (DIRECTOR OF PHOTOGRAPHY). I believe Images capture a moment in time that you can never replicate.

*TASK: KEEP A CAMERA AT HAND IN ORDER TO TAKE PHOTOGRAPHS AND/OR FILMS IN ANY MOMENT. IN SPONTANEOUS MOMENTS IS WHERE CREATIVITY AND MAGIC COME TO LIFE. WHEN RECORDED YOU CAN RETAIN THESE HAPPY MOMENTS FOR LIFE... NRD

"Since I'm inarticulate, I express myself with images." Helen Levitt

"To me, movies and music go hand in hand. When I'm writing a script, one of the first things I do is find the music I'm going to play for the opening sequence." QUENTIN TARANTINO

"Now more than ever we need to talk to each other, to listen to each other and understand how we see the world, and cinema is the best medium for doing this." MARTIN SCORCESE

"Nature is so powerful, so strong. Capturing its essence is not easy - your work becomes a dance with light and the weather. It takes you to a place within yourself." Annie Leibovitz

"Chic is nothing but the right nothing."
Mario Testino

BARRY MCCALL PHOTOGRAPHY:
http://www.barrymccallphotographer.com/

PILATES

Pilates's founder, Joseph Hubert Pilates states "Never an aspirin. Never injured a day in my life. The whole country, the whole world, should be doing my exercises. They'd be happier. Everything should be smooth, like a cat. [The exercises are done lying, sitting, kneeling, etc.] to avoid excess strain on the heart and lungs... natural movements with the emphasis on doing and being."

PLAY TO WIN...

*PLAY TO WIN IN LIFE:
- BE CREATIVE IN EVERY MOMENT.
- NEVER DECIDE TO BE A VICTIM.
- A HERO IS DOWN TO A DECISION.

- A VICTIM ACTS ON IMPULSES.
- A HERO ACTS ON INNER CALM, IN THE MOMENT-OVERCOMES OBSTACLES IN BALANCE AND CREATIVELY. THEREFORE, ALWAYS SHINES IN THE END.

*WHICH OPTION WILL YOU TAKE?

POETRY

"Poetry may make us from time to time a little more aware of the deeper, unnamed feelings which form the substratum of our being, to which we rarely penetrate: for our lives are mostly a constant evasion of ourselves." T. S. Eliot

"Poetry is nearer to vital truth than history." Plato

"Poetry is when an emotion has found its thought and the thought has found words." Robert Frost

POSITIVITY

POSITIVITY IS THE ONLY WAY TO LIVE. FOCUS ON **WHAT YOU CAN DO!** WHY TALK ABOUT WHAT YOU CAN'T? IT IS A WASTE YOUR TIME. **INSTEAD USE THIS TIME TO CREATE POSITIVE SOLUTIONS.** IF YOU ARE POSITIVE YOU WILL ATTRACT THIS… WATCH THIS SPACE! NRD

"A pessimist sees the difficulty in every opportunity: an optimist sees the opportunity in every difficulty." Winston Churchill

"I FEEL GOOD...
I KNEW THAT I WOULD NOW...
SO GOOD,
SO GOOD." JAMES BROWN

PRESSURE

PRESSURE ON YOURSELF OR OTHERS
IS NEVER GOING TO HELP ANY
SITUATION.
YOU CONTROL YOUR PRESSURE GAUGE.
LET THE AIR OUT,
LET THE PRESSURE GO...
LIVE AND ENJOY NOW.

PROMISES

EACH PERSON KNOWS THEIR OWN VALUES.
YET, OFTEN WHEN OFF BALANCE WE NEGATE
AWAY FROM THESE. SO, I HAVE SET OUT A
LIST OF DAILY PROMISES TO REMIND
YOURSELF OF THESE VALUES. THESE ARE
USEFUL MOSTLY IN TIMES OF STRESS.

NO RULES: YOU MAY READ THESE DAILY.
WEEKLY OR MONTHLY. TO START, I HAVE
WRITTEN SOME BUT PLEASE DO RE-WRITE
THESE AND/OR CREATE YOUR OWN. AIM:
LIVE IN EACH MOMENT IN BALANCE.

DAILY PROMISES:

◊ I DESERVE TO BE HAPPY AND IN BALANCE.

◊ EVERYONE I MEET AND KNOW DESERVES TO BE HAPPY AND BALANCED.

◊ I WISH TO LIVE IN THE MOMENT AND EMBRACE EACH DAY.

◊ I WILL NOT BASE MY HAPPINESS ON THE MOODS OR FEELINGS OF OTHERS.

◊ I AM UNIQUE AND ACCEPT THIS AS MY STRENGTH.

◊ I REALISE THAT MY ENERGY AFFECTS BOTH OTHERS AND MYSELF. SO, I WILL TAKE RESPONSIBILITY FOR THIS EACH DAY AND FOCUS ON POSITIVE ENERGY IN EACH MOMENT.

◊ I WILL REPLACE ANY NEGATIVE THOUGHTS WITH POSITVE ONES.

◊ I CAN CREATE ANYTHING I WISH TO FOR IN MY LIFE, ONCE I HAVE FAITH AND EMRACE THE MOMENT.

◊ I WILL ONLY ALLOW PEOPLE IN MY LIFE THAT ACCEPT ME FOR ME. AS I WILL.

◊ I WILL ACCEPT THAT PEOPLE I MEET ARE PART OF JOURNEY. IT IS UP TO ME TO DECIDE WHAT THEIR LESSON IS TO ME, WHETHER THEY ARE MEANT TO REMAIN OR NOT IN MY LIFE.

◊ I DESERVE TO SMILE AND LAUGH EACH DAY. AS DO ALL.

◊ I HAVE THE CONFIDENCE TO FIGHT MY FEARS.

◊ I KNOW THAT PAIN IS PART OF MY JOURNEY AND I WILL EMBRACE IT AND LET IT GO. YET, I WILL NOT ACCEPT CONTINUOUS PAIN THAT STOPS ME ON MY PATH.

◊ I MUST BE MYSELF IN EACH DAY AND ALLOW MYSELF, AND OTHERS THE FREEDOM TO GROW EACH DAY.

◊ I ALWAYS HAVE OPTIONS. I WILL LISTEN TO MY INTUITION AND CHOSE THE RIGHT ONES FOR ME IN THE MOMENT.

◊ I WILL ASK FOR HELP AND KNOW THAT I AM STRONG EVEN IF I ASK FOR HELP.

◊ I WILL WRITE DOWN MY THOUGHTS AND IDEAS AT LEAST ONCE A WEEK. THEN PUT THESE INTO ACTION OR LET THEM GO…I NEED SPACE TO ENJOY NOW.

◊ I WILL CHERISH MY HEALTH.

◊ I WILL NOT PITY OR JUDGE OTHERS AS I KNOW IT IS ONLY MY EGO JUDGING OTHERS.

◊ I WILL PLAN FOR TOMORROW, CHERISH MY PAST BUT ALWAYS LIVE FOR NOW ☺

PSYCHOTHERAPY

Everyone has times in their lives that they may need some added support and a trusted and trained professional seems suited. Some people wish for a private space to let it all out and let go. The aim should be to speak, listen to advice, let go, move on with the aim to live for now.

TASK: EMBRACE YOUR SENSITIVITY. TALK IT OUT…FIND WAYS TO CHANNEL THIS INTO CREATIVITY-MAGIC WILL HAPPEN ☺

According to www.webmd.com, psychotherapy/therapy involves talking with a licensed health care practitioner to identify and work through factors contributing to one's illness. The following are the 3 main types of psychotherapy: Psychodynamic Therapy, Interpersonal Therapy and Cognitive-Behavioral Therapy:

1. Psychodynamic therapy views the illness as stemming from unresolved, unconscious conflicts, often from childhood.

2. Interpersonal therapy focuses on a patient's behaviors and interactions with family and friends.

3. Cognitive-behavioral therapy helps one identify and change inaccurate perceptions one has of self and the world.

PURPOSE

WE ALL HAVE A 'TRUE PURPOSE', WHICH MAY VARY AT DIFFERING TIMES OF OUR LIVES. YET, IT IS UP TO YOU TO LOOK INSIDE AND FIND THIS.
THEN LIVE IT. HONOUR YOUR PURPOSE, (EVEN IF IT SCARES YOU).

IT IS TIED TO YOUR HAPPINESS AND BALANCE. IT WILL EVOLVE-BE OPEN. THE WORLD NEEDS YOU TO SHARE YOUR PURPOSE WITH OTHERS… WHAT'S YOURS? NRD

"Our purpose in each other's lives: to invoke each other's greatness and work a miracle in each other's lives." Marianne Williamson

"You have to find what sparks a light in you so that you in your own way can illuminate the world."
Oprah Winfrey

Questions...

"The questions which one asks oneself begin, at last, to illuminate the world and become one's key to the experience of others." James Baldwin, U.S. writer

"You've got the words to change a nation,
But you're biting you tongue...
So afraid you'll say something wrong...
If no one ever hears it,
How we gonna learn your song?
SO, COME ON, COME ON..." Emeli Sandé

QUESTIONS FOR YOU:
◊ WHAT/WHO MAKES ME HAPPY?
◊ WHAT SKILLS ARE NATURAL TO ME?
◊ HOW DO I KEEP MY BALANCE?
◊ WHAT ARE MY GOALS OR DREAMS?
◊ HOW CAN I CREATE MY GOALS OR DREAMS?
◊ WHAT HOLDS ME BACK IN MY GOALS? WHY?
◊ HOW CAN I ENJOY MY LIFE MORE EACH DAY?
◊ HOW CAN I BE MORE POSITIVE? BALANCED?
◊ WHAT HELPS ME TO LIVE IN THE MOMENT?

ASK YOURSELF AS MANY QUESTIONS AS YOU WISH.
AIM: TO FIND YOUR WAY TO LIVE IN BALANCE...

* TIME TO WRITE YOUR STORY

Reading

PLEASE BE CAUTIOUS OF WHAT YOU READ. THIS WILL GO INTO YOUR CONSCIOUSNESS AND EFFECT YOUR DAILY INTERACTIONS, MOODS AND OPINIONS. FOCUS ON READING POSITIVE, CREATIVE AND BALANCED WRITING-THIS WILL INSPIRE YOU.

"Reading is to the mind what exercise is to the body."
Richard Steele

REFLEXOLOGY

The Reflexology Association of Canada defines reflexology as: "A natural healing art based on the principle that there are reflexes in the feet, hands and ears and their referral areas which correspond to every part, gland and organ of the body. Through application of pressure on these reflexes without tools or lotions, the feet being the primary area of application, reflexology relieves tension, improves circulation and helps promote the natural function of the related areas of the body."

REIKI

The word Reiki (pronounced Ray-Key) is a Japanese kanji for universal life-force energy. According to the Canadian Reiki Association; "Reiki is a Japanese holistic, light-touch, energy-based modality. Working as a support mechanism to the body, Reiki re-establishes a normal energy flow of ki (life force energy) throughout the system, which in turn can enhance and accelerate the body's innate healing ability.

Through a series of hand positions either directly on or just above the body, the energy worker allows for the flow of energy through their body. The client's body then draws off the amount of energy that is required. The simplicity of a Reiki session may raise some skepticism, however, after experiencing it, many clients keep coming back for more of those relaxing feelings."

RELATE

TRY TO RELATE TO OTHERS… IT MAKES LIFE EASIER IF YOU RELATE.

"Anything that you resent and strongly react to in another is also in you."
Eckhart Tolle

RELATIONSHIPS

*IN RELATIONSHIPS, YOU MUST BE THE PARTNER YOU WISH TO FIND…

Q. HOW CAN YOU EXPECT RESPECT, BALANCE, LOVE AND LIGHT IF YOU ARE NOT WILLING TO SHARE THESE QUALITIES WITH YOUR PARTNER? *RELATIONSHIPS ARE MEANT TO ENHANCE YOUR LIFE.

N.B. 'IN LOVE' or life, if your partner or anyone in your life tries to make you jealous or plays games with you…
PLEASE IGNORE THEM and remember it is
THEIR BLOCK, NOT YOURS:

- DETACH FROM THEIR DRAMA.
- IF YOU DON'T GIVE THEM ATTENTION, EVENTUALLY THEY WILL STOP AS THEY WILL REALISE YOU'RE NOT BUYING INTO IT.
- *DRAMA IS A CRY FOR ATTENTION. ALWAYS TRY TO HELP SOMEONE IF THEY NEED HELP.
- YET, IF THEY WON'T HELP THEMSELVES THEN DETACH AS IS NOT YOUR PROBLEM.
- YOU DESERVE RESPECT AND BALANCE.
- LIFE IS TOO SHORT FOR DRAMA…
- DON'T WASTE YOUR TIME IN LIFE OR LOVE.
- KEEP LIFE SIMPLE.
- KEEP LOVE SIMPLE.
- LOVE LIFE.
- LOVE LOVE. NRD.

RELIGION

EACH RELIGION HAS ONE SIMILAR GOAL=FAITH. PEOPLE JUDGE RELIGIONS EASILY. SO, I HAVE SHARED SOME AWARENESS ON RELIGIONS…

*YOU DO NOT NEED TO BELIEVE IN ANOTHER FAITH. YET, UNLESS SOMEONE IS HARMING YOU OR YOUR FAMILY, WHAT OTHERS BELIEVE IS THEIR RIGHT. SO, ALLOW OTHERS THE FREEDOM TO BELIEVE.

Atheism: Atheists are people who believe that god or gods are man-made constructs. They have a disbelief in the existence of a supreme being or beings.

Baha'i: A religion founded in Iran in 1863 by Husayn ʿAlī (called Bahaullah) teaching the essential worth of all religions, the unity of all races, and the equality of the sexes.

Buddhism: originated in India by Buddha (Gautama) and later spreading to China, Burma, Japan, Tibet, and parts of southeast Asia, holding that life is full of suffering caused by desire and that the way to end this suffering is through enlightenment that enables one to halt the endless sequence of births and deaths to which one is otherwise subject.

Candomblé: based on the worship of Yoruba deities, practiced in Brazil, especially in the state of Bahia.

Christianity: The world's biggest faith, based on the teaching of Jesus Christ. This includes the Catholic, Protestant, and Eastern Orthodox churches.

Hinduism: A group of faiths rooted in the religious ideas of India, based upon the religion of the original Aryan settlers as expounded and evolved in the Vedas, the Upanishads, the Bhagavad-Gita, etc., having an extremely diversified character with many schools of philosophy and theology, and a large pantheon symbolizing the many attributes of a single god.

Islam: Revealed in its final form by the Prophet Muhammad and taught by the Koran, the basic principle of which is absolute submission to a unique and personal god, Allah.

Jainism: An ancient philosophy and ethical teaching that originated in India, founded in the 6th century B.C. as a revolt against Hinduism and emphasizing the perfectibility of human nature and liberation of the soul, especially through asceticism and nonviolence toward all living creatures.

Jehovah's Witnesses: A Christian-based evangelistic religious movement founded in the U.S. in the late 19th century. This believes in the imminent destruction of the world's wickedness and the establishment of a theocracy under God's rule.

Judaism: Based around the Jewish people's covenant relationship with God. the monotheistic religion of the Jews, having its ethical, ceremonial, and legal foundation in the precepts of the Old Testament and in the teachings and commentaries of the rabbis as found chiefly in the Talmud. There are various types; Conservative Jew, Orthodox and Reform Jew.

Mormonism: The Church of Jesus Christ of Latter-day Saints, believed to be an abridgment by a prophet (Mormon) of a record of certain ancient peoples in America, written on golden plates, and discovered and translated (1827-30) by Joseph Smith.

Paganism: Contemporary religions usually based on reverence for nature, a community observing a polytheistic religion, as the ancient Romans and Greeks.

Rastafari: A young religion founded in Jamaica in the 1930s, that regards Africa as the Promised Land, to which all true believers will someday return, and the late Haile Selassie I, former emperor of Ethiopia, as the messiah.

Santeria: Afro-Caribbean syncretic religion originating in Cuba. This merges the worship of Yoruba deities with veneration of Roman Catholic saints: practiced in Cuba and spread to other parts of the Caribbean and to the U.S. by Cuban emigrés.

Shinto: Japanese folk tradition and ritual with no founder or single sacred scripture based on the idea of embracing nature.

Sikhism: The religion founded by Guru Nanak in India in the 15th Century CE. that refuses to recognize the Hindu caste system or the Brahmanical priesthood and forbids magic, idolatry, and pilgrimages.

Spiritualism: Spiritualists believe in communication with the spirits of people who have died. They can and do communicate with the living, especially through a person (a medium) particularly susceptible to their influence.

Taoism: An ancient tradition of philosophy and belief rooted in Chinese worldview. The philosophical system evolved by Lao-tzu and Chuang-Tzu. It advocates a life of complete simplicity and naturalness and of noninterference with the course of natural events, in order to attain a happy existence in harmony with the Tao.

Unitarianism: An open-minded and individualistic approach to religion. A North American liberal religious denomination in the Judeo-Christian heritage, formed in 1961 by the merger of the Unitarians, organized in 1825, and the Universalists, organized in 1793.

Zoroastrianism: One of the oldest monotheistic faiths, founded by the Prophet Zoroaster. an Iranian religion, founded c600 B.C. by Zoroaster, the principal beliefs of which are in the existence of a supreme deity, Ahura Mazda, and in a cosmic struggle between a spirit of good, Spenta Mainyu, and a spirit of evil, Angra Mainyu.

REST

YOU MUST REST.
'REST' DEPENDS ON EACH INDIVIDUAL.
PLEASE STOP WHEN YOU NEED REST.
BALANCE ALLOWS FOR REST IN LIFE.
*FIND YOUR OWN WAY TO SWITCH OFF.

PAMPER ROOM

FIND YOUR TIME TO REST_NRD

RESPECT

- RESPECT YOURSELF.
- RESPECT YOUR HEALTH.
- RESPECT OTHERS.
- RESPECT LIFE.
- RESPECT LOVE.
- RESPECT EACH DAY.
- *RESPECT YOUR FAMILY AND THE ELDERLY- THIS SHOWS DEPTH IN A CHARACTER.

Self

BE YOUR-**SELF!** EVERYDAY. LIFE IS PRECIOUS. YOU ARE WONDERFUL, JUST AS YOU ARE.

"Make the most of yourself for that is all there is."
Ralph Waldo Emerson

"In order to bring the individuation process into reality, one must surrender consciously to the power of unconscious, instead of thinking in terms of what one should do, or of what is generally though right, or what usually happens. One must simply listen, in order to learn what the inner totality-the self-wants one to do here and now in a particular situation." Carl Jung

QUESTION TIME (ESPECIALLY FOR WOMEN)

Q. WHO CREATED 'SIZE 0' OR BEAUTIFUL=SKINNY IMAGE OR MUSCLES=MASCULINE CONCEPT?

A. WHO REALLY CARES?!

IF YOU ARE NATURALLY SLIM, BE SLIM.
IF YOU ARE NATURALLY MUSCULAR, BE MUSCULAR.

*IF YOU ARE NOT SIZE 0 OR 'IN FASHION', THEN LET IT GO.
REMEMBER YOU ARE FANTASTIC-AS YOU ARE.
EMBRACE YOU AS YOU ARE.
TAKE AWAY THIS UNNECESSARY PRESSURE.
IT IS A FAÇADE!

- *YET, IF YOU ARE UNHAPPY WITH YOUR HEALTH OR BODY IMAGE…THEN WORK ON IT TODAY. THE TIME IS NOW.
- TAKE EXERCISE: WALK TO WORK, WALK YOUR KIDS, TAKE CLASSES, CREATE A RUNNING CLUB WITH FRIENDS…

- EAT IN BALANCE-OR TRY ☺
- ASK FOR SUPPORT TO GET YOU STARTED.
- BALANCE IS A DAILY PROGRAMME.
- YOUR HEALTH IS ALWAYS
  A PRIORITY.

YET, THIS 'IMAGE PATTERN' IS
HURTING AND PRESSURING SO
MANY PEOPLE WORLDWIDE.
BEAUTY IS NOT FORCED.
BEAUTY IS BEING YOUR TRUE
SELF IN EACH DAY.

-THERE IS NOW A WAR ON IMAGE-
PLEASE REMEMBER,
NO ONE WINS IN A WAR!!!
SO, STOP FIGHTING AGAINST YOURSELF.
YOU ARE GREAT, JUST AS YOU ARE.
BE HAPPY IN YOUR BODY.
IT IS YOUR BIGGEST GIFT-CHERISH IT.

LET NO ONE (YOURSELF INCLUDED) TELL
YOU THAT YOU NEED TO BE ANY SIZE OR
SHAPE OTHER THAN WHAT YOU ARE.
*IF   THEY   DO,   IT   IS   THEIR
INSECURITY/BLOCK, NOT YOURS!

BE YOU.
BE BEAUTIFUL.
IT STARTS WITHIN.
START LIVING BEAUTIFUL.
START LIVING BALANCE.
START NOW. NRD

SELF-IMAGE AND STYLE

- *YOUR STYLE SHOULD BE TRUE TO YOU.
- *NOT SEEN AS AN 'IMAGE OF YOU'!
- *HOW YOU DRESS IS THE FIRST
  INDICATION OF YOUR SELF-IMAGE AND
  AWARENESS OF YOURSELF.
- WE ALL HAVE TRIALS AND ERRORS
  GROWING UP. YET, DRESS AS YOU NOW.

- *YOU WILL LOOK AND FEEL YOUR BEST IF YOU ARE TRUE TO YOUR OWN STYLE.
- *NEVER FORGET, HOW YOU DRESS IS ABOUT THE ENERGY YOU WISH TO SHARE WITH OTHERS.
- *PLEASE BE CAUTIOUS OF THIS ENERGY EXCHANGE-CHERISH YOUR ENERGY. NRD

SENSITIVITY

- SENSITIVITY IS MY ESSENCE. IN EACH DAY AND MOMENT I HONOUR THIS. I DISLIKE THE MISCONCEPTION THAT SENSITIVE PEOPLE ARE WEAK-QUITE THE CONTRARY. SENSITIVITY AND STRENGTH ARE INEXTRICABLY LINKED.

- EACH PERSON HAS SENSITIVITY YET, MOST PEOPLE BLOCK IT DUE TO THIS STEREOTYPE. WHAT A PITY!

- IN LIFE, SENSITIVITY ALLOWS FOR AN ATTENTION TO DETAIL, SENSITIVTY TO OTHERS AND AN APPRECIATION FOR BEAUTY IN THE SIMPLICITY OF LIFE.

- IN MY WORK MY SENSITIVITY PERVADES. IN COMMUNICATONS AND INTERACTIONS WITH PEOPLE IT IS NECESSARY. ALSO, IN DESIGN IT IS IMPERATIVE, AS DESIGN REQUIRES ATTENTION TO EACH DETAIL AND WHEN MET, REACHES ALL OF YOUR SENSES IN THE MOST IMPACTFUL WAY. MOST IMPORTANTLY, BRINGING YOU INTO NOW.

- TASK: EMBRACE YOUR OWN SENSITIVITY AND CHANNEL IT INTO SOMETHING CREATIVE.

TASK: PLEASE HONOUR SENSITIVITY IN YOU AND OTHERS. BE SENSITIVE OF/TO THE PEOPLE AROUND YOU IN EACH DAY. IN YOUR RELATIONSHIPS, FAMILY, WORK AND LIFE… BE SENSITIVE TO OTHER PEOPLE'S FEELINGS AND ENERGY.

ESPECIALLY WITH PEOPLE YOU JUST MEET- YOU DO NOT KNOW WHAT IS GOING ON IN SOMEONE ELSE'S LIFE… ACKNOWLEDGE THAT.

*PLEASE DON'T PROJECT YOUR STRESS OR NEGATIVE ENERGY ONTO OTHERS. EQUALLY, DON'T ALLOW OTHERS PROJECT NEGATIVE ENERGY ONTO YOU. SENSITIVITY=BALANCE.

"The best things in life are unseen, that is why we close our eyes when we kiss, cry and dream." Unknown.

SENSITIVITY = ←------
STRENGTH + |
SENSITIVITY = |
STRENGTH   ←------

SERENDIPITY AND SYNCHRONICITY

"Coincidences are spiritual puns."
G.K. Chesterton (1874 - 1936)

"Synchronicity reveals the meaningful connections between the subjective and objective world." Carl G. Jung (1875 - 1961)

SERVICE

"Service to others is the rent you pay for your room here on earth." Muhammad Ali

"The best way to find yourself is to lose yourself in the service of others."
Mahatma Gandhi

SILENCE

Nowadays, silence is rare. People pay vast amounts to go on retreats in order to have this space. Silence is something that should be honoured as part of your balance. It must be a daily practice to find your silence.
Whether it is in the car or walking to work or before sleeping. Silence is key to calm.

*How can you ever evolve or create if every moment is filled with noise?

TASK: FIND YOUR SILENT SPACE IN EACH MOMENT. EVEN IN NOISE… WORK OUT A WAY WHERE YOU CAN HAVE SILENCE.

"Silence is so accurate."
Mark Rothko

"God is the friend of silence.
See how nature-trees, flowers, grass-grows in silence:
see the stars, the moon and the sun, how they move in silence...
We need silence to be able to touch souls."
Mother Teresa (1910-1997)

SIMPLICITY

"As you simplify your life, the laws of the universe will be simpler: solitude will not be solitude, poverty will not be poverty, nor weakness weakness." Henry David Thoreau

"Simplicity makes me happy." Alicia Keys

BE YOU. KEEP LIFE SIMPLE. Nrd

SLEEP

SLEEP IS KEY TO BALANCE.
EVERYTHING IS BETTER AFTER GOOD SLEEP.
SLEEP WELL.

SMILE

"There are a variety of smiles.

Some smiles are sarcastic. Some smiles are artificial-diplomatic smiles.
These smiles do not produce satisfaction, but rather fear or suspicion… But a genuine smile gives us hope, freshness. If we want a genuine smile, then first we must produce the basis for a smile to come."
Dalai Lama

SOULMATE

One of my favourite subjects is Classical Studies. I am fascinated by Greek and Roman mythology. It is a matter of opinion whether you believe or not but there are stories such as the idea of a 'soulmate', which relates to now.
*I believe happiness and love must be within you to find love outside of you. Yet, I embrace the idea of a 'soulmate' being the person who balances you and you balancing them-to me this is essence of true love. NRD

NOW, each day people all around the world are on a search to find a 'Soulmate' so you might want to know where it stemmed from…"In 380 BCE, Plato, below, described how soulmates came to be in *The Origin of Soulmates as Revealed in The Symposium:* In 'The Symposium" people weren't what we consider "normal" as they were two people sharing the same body. Hence, these individuals were extremely powerful, so powerful that Zeus and the other Gods feared their strength. Trouble arose when the Gods heard that these beings they created were thinking about climbing to heaven to replace the gods.

However, Zeus, patient and wise, listened to their malicious plans and came up with one of his own. He proposed they cut these human beings in half. This would benefit the gods in many ways. First, it would double the number of people making offerings to the gods. Secondly, it would weaken the race, cutting their strength in half.

All the gods loved the idea and the humans were divided in two. Inevitably, the human race was confused, upset and feeling empty. Zeus, was filled with compassion and made a decision to allow them to find happiness or 'oneness' in their ability to bond intimately and pro-create.

Since that day, the human race has been in search of their soul mate and when they do find them it is the feeling is of oneness and balance."

SPIRITUALITY

SPIRITUALITY IS HAVING AN OPEN MIND TO THE WORLD, PRACTICES AND PEOPLE: TODAY. NRD

SPACE

PLEASE ALLOW SPACE IN YOUR LIFE FOR NEW ENERGY, PEOPLE AND POSSIBILITIES. HOW DO YOU EXPECT TO HAVE CHANGE, GROWTH OR CREATE IF THERE IS NO ROOM FOR THIS IN YOUR LIFE?

Task: CLEAR YOUR LIFE OF ANY NEGATIVE OR UNNECESSARY SPACE.
Clear out your wardrobe and home of any clutter (donate to charity).
Clear your calendar for free time
Clear your mind of any idle thoughts.
ALLOW ROOM FOR POSITIVE SPACE IN LIFE.

SPORT

"Through my fathers' career I realize the power of sports, on every level. Having seen my dad play for Ireland and various other teams, then continue to coach, I share a passion for sport, health and fitness.

Yet, I also see sport as a medium of connecting people and breaking negative boundaries in societies across the world...

Personally, having worked for the 'League of Ireland Football League', and many events for Ski, Snowboarding and Freerunning championships in London. Along with, working on campaigns in Ireland for: Special Olympics, 'Sports Against Racism (SARI)' and 'Show Racism the Red Card', I know that sports can break boundaries: Race, religion, creed and class. It unites all.

Whether it is a school team, The Olympics or The Super bowl, the power of such an array of people for one event or union of Sport is immeasurable." Natasha Rocca Devine

"Sport in whatever form it takes, offers several positives to all its participants. To some it provides fun and entertainment away from the stresses of work or everyday life. To others at the professional levels, it can take people to the greatest highs and the worst lows in victory and defeat. Sport exposes its participants to a broad range of human emotions." John Devine

"I never cry about what I don't have. I'm always positive. I am happy with the team I have and I am confident that we can do well." Fabio Capello, Italian football (soccer) coach

"I have always tried to be the bridge between the club and the fans and I have tried to support the fans in a lot of their pleas and causes." Alex Ferguson, Coach of Manchester United Football (soccer) Club

"Champions aren't made in the gyms. Champions are made from something they have deep inside them -- a desire, a dream, a vision." Muhammad Ali

"Love is playing every game as if it's your last." Michael Jordan

"Sport is a preserver of health."
Hippocrates

START

START OFF EACH DAY, JOB, RELATIONSHIP AS YOU
MEAN TO CONTINUE…
ALWAYS POSITIVE
AND IN BALANCE
AND IN THE MOMENT.
Natasha Rocca Devine

STEP BACK

"SOMETIMES YOU NEED TO STEP BACK, ACKNOWLEDGE THINGS FROM THE BIGGER PICTURE.
ALWAYS REMEMBER TO SMILE.
GET BACK INTO THE MOMENT. POSITIVE SOLUTIONS WILL COME ONLY IN A POSITIVE SPACE. Nrd

STILLNESS

"Man is ill because he is never still." Paracelsus

"Within you there is a stillness and a sanctuary to which you can retreat at any time and be yourself." Hermann Hesse

"It is the stillness that will save and transform the world." Eckhart Tolle

STRENGTH

The concept of strength is difficult to measure and has varying degrees. For men and women and differing ages and cultures it differs. Yet, the key factor for me is the ability to embrace each moment. It is about not giving up, even when you wish to.

LOOK INSIDE YOU AND NEVER FORGET THAT YOU HAVE THE STRENGTH TO OVERCOME ANYTHING THAT COMES YOUR WAY.

"AS YOU THINK, SO SHALL YOU BECOME."

BRUCE LEE

"We never know how high we are
Till we are called to rise:
And then, if we are true to plan,
Our statures touch the skies."
Emily Dickinson

STOP

PLEASE...
◊ STOP LOOKING FOR APPROVAL-YOU WILL NEVER PLEASE ALL. SO, APPROVE OF YOURSELF ALONE.

◇ STOP SEARCHING FOR A BETTER VERSION OF WHAT YOU HAVE-BE HAPPY FOR ALL THAT YOU HAVE.

◇ STOP EXPLAINING YOURSELF-JUST BE YOU.

◇ STOP LIVING IN THE PAST OR THE FUTURE-LIVE FOR NOW.

◇ STOP DEFINING YOURSELF-ACCEPT THAT YOU WILL CHANGE SO GIVE YOURSELF FREEDOM TO DO SO.

◇ STOP PLAYING A VICTIM-YOU ARE A HERO. YOU DESERVE TO BE.

◇ STOP NEGLECTING YOUR HEALTH: BODY AND MIND-YOU NEED YOUR HEALTH FOR BALANCE AND HAPPINESS.

◊ STOP PLAYING GAMES IN LIFE AND LOVE-HONOUR LOVE. HONOUR LIFE.

◊ STOP CONTROLLING OR TRYING TO CONTROL YOURSELF, EVERYTHING AND EVERYONE IN YOUR LIFE-EMBRACE NOW, LET GO...

◊ STOP BLAMING OTHERS IN LIFE-EVERYTHING YOU WISH FOR IS CREATED ONLY BY YOU.

◊ STOP SCREAMING-BEING HEARD REQUIRES CALM COMMUNICATION.

◊ PLEASE STOP BLOCKING YOURSELF...
◊ START LIVING THE LIFE YOU DESERVE!
◊ YOU ARE ENTITLED TO BE HAPPY.
◊ START TODAY. START NOW. NRD

STRESS

SAY NO TO STRESS.
DON'T CREATE IT.
DEFLATE IT!

"The major cause of stress is the inability of people to discover their real nature. Discover your gifts, follow them and you will never feel stressed." Pavel Stoyanov

SUCCESS

"Don't let a mad world tell you that **success is anything other than a successful present moment.**"
Eckhart Tolle

"If everyone is moving forward together, then success takes care of itself."
Henry Ford

"KNOW THAT THERE IS ENOUGH ROOM FOR EVERYONE

TO BE PASSIONATE,CREATIVE AND SUCCESSUL.

IN FACT, THERE IS MORE THAN ENOUGH ROOM FOR EVERYONE.

THERE IS A NEED FOR EVERYONE."

MARIANNE WILLIAMSON.

*Q and A:

"How do YOU define success?"
MOMENT OF TRUTH: Will this success aid your Health? Security? Happiness? Balance? Love? Light?
OR add stress, pressure etc. on you???

*TRUE SUCCESS=BALANCE.

SUNLIGHT

Sunlight and light gives energy and adds balance in life. Growing up in Ireland, it was not always easy to have constant sunlight. Yet, each day going outside even for a walk is imperative. As even in dark times, there is always serotonin in the skies…

*Find your sunlight in each day.

"Those who bring sunshine into the lives of others cannot keep it from themselves." James M. Barrie

SURRENDER

SURRENDER TO NOW. NRD.

Teach and Teaching

- TEACHERS IN SCHOOLS, COLLEGES ETC. ARE LEADERS IN LIFE, ESPECIALLY WITH CHILDREN, THEY PLAY A KEY ROLE IN SHAPING THEIR LIVES. HENCE, THEIR BALANCE AND AWARENESS IS ESSENTIAL.
- EVERYONE HAS THE ABILITY TO TEACH.
- TEACH YOURSELF AND SHARE WITH OTHERS WHAT MATTERS TO YOU.
- TEACHING EXTENDS TO ALL AND IS PART OF DAILY LIFE.
- TEACHING MEANS SHARING INFORMATION BUT ALSO GIVING PEOPLE THE FREEDOM TO HAVE AN OPINION DIFFERENT TO YOURS.
- IT IS NOT FORCE BUT CREATIVE.
- TEACHING=AWARENESS=EMBRACING NOW NATASHA ROCCA DEVINE

"Teaching is the highest form of understanding." Aristotle

"We cannot teach people anything: we can only help them discover it within themselves." Galileo Galilei

TEAMS-IN LIFE

Unbeknown to ourselves, we are all part of a larger 'team' on a small and vaster scale. It is clear with the internet and technology that we are all interconnected. Whether we accept this or not is immaterial. As history proves, one person can impact the world both negatively and positively. So, in a team each person is inextricably linked to the effects of the other member(s). Now, the results are immediate. The power is immeasurable.

Hence, it takes only one person to make a difference to the overall dynamic. So, even amidst chaos or times of pressure, if one persons' balance and strength remains intact, this will benefit the others. This responsibility for your inner authority is so powerful that you alone have the power to make a change.

Whether it is online, in work, in a friendship, intimate relationship or a team, your balance will have a positive ripple effect on both yourself, and others each day of your life. REALISE THE POWER YOU POSSESS WITHIN. REALSE THAT THE POSITIVE CHANGE STARTS WITH YOU!!!

"Ask not what your teammates can do for you. Ask what you can do for your teammates." Magic Johnson-American NBA basketball star.

THOUGHTS

EMBRACE YOUR THOUGHTS IN EACH MOMENT. WRITE THEM, SPEAK THEM, PAINT THEM, ACT THEM…
THEN PUT THEM INTO ACTION OR SET THEM FREE.

"We get into the habit of living before acquiring the habit of thinking. In that race which daily hastens us towards death, the body maintains its irreparable lead." Albert Camus

"As long as you're going to think anyway, think big."
Donald Trump

"If you don't like something, change it: if you can't change it, change the way you think about it." Mary Engelbreit

"Nurture your mind with great thoughts for you will never go higher than you think." Benjamin Disraeli

"Trouble is inevitable, misery is optional."
Joel Esteen, Pastor

"Seek not to change the world but to change your mind about the world.

What you see reflects your thinking. Your thinking reflects your choice of what you want to see."

Taken from *"A Course in Miracles", Marianne Williamson*

TIME

Time allows us to make plans and be committed in each day. Yet, in order to live for now, you must let go of 'physical time' as you cannot prepare for what is ahead. You must plan and be present in the moment but allow for spontaneity. This is the essence of living time. EACH DAY IS AN ADVENTURE WHEN YOU DON'T KNOW WHAT IS AHEAD ☺

"Dost thou love life? Then do not squander time, for that is the stuff life is made of." Benjamin Franklin

TRAVEL

Working, studying and living all around the world has given me a deeper Awareness of the world and people of all cultures. Yet, it was mostly in Asia, Egypt and South America was where I moved beyond words. Whilst in South America and Thailand I was met with many children living on the street. It was clear that they were struggling without any support and seeing these innocent children vulnerable upset me greatly. I wished to do something to help them...

Yet, each child continued to smile and embodied a sense of fearlessness. I was in awe of their Awareness. They had no option but to find their inner strength within each day for survival.

This way of living inspired me greatly. They reminded me that living for now, without fear or ego is the best option in life.

TRIBE

I CALL ALL THOSE IN MY CLOSE CIRCLE-MY TRIBE.
YET, WE ARE ALL CONNECTED.
WE ARE ALL PART OF A LARGER TRIBE
(ONLINE/GLOBALLY).
HONOUR YOURSELF,
HONOUR YOUR TRIBE.
HONOUR EACH TRIBE. NRD.

"Prejudice comes from being in the dark: sunlight disinfects it."
Muhammad Ali

TRUST

TRUST IN YOUR INSTINCTS.
TRUST OTHERS.
LET GO OF THE PAST.
TRUST IN EVERYTHING TODAY!

TRUTH

"The voice of truth speaks to every person on the planet every day and is as loud as we are willing to listen."
Gandhi

"We become so full once we make ourselves empty:
We become so smart once we realize we're not and
We become so powerful once
We understand we're priceless." Marianne Williamson

TRUTH IS RIGHT IN FRONT OF US.
EVERYDAY PEOPLE SHOW US THEIR TRUTH
BUT WE MUST ACCEPT IT…
IT IS ALSO WITHIN US.
SO, EACH DAY.
LIVE TRUTH.
ALWAYS SPEAK TRUTH.
ONLY ACCEPT TRUTH.
BE TRUTH. Natasha Rocca Devine

Understand

UNDERSTAND YOURSELF.

UNDERSTAND OTHERS AROUND YOU.

IF YOU CAN'T UNDERSTAND THEM, THEN ACCEPT THEM AND THEIR DIFFERENCES.

UNDERSTAND THAT EACH DAY IS AN ADVENTURE TO CONQUER.

UNDERSTAND YOUR SIGNIFICANCE IN THE BIGGER PICTURE.

UNDERSTAND THE POWER OF EACH MOMENT.

UNDERSTAND THE POWER YOU HAVE IN EACH MOMENT SO LIVE AND ENJOY NOW.

"IT IS NOT ONLY SEEING THE BEAUTY IN THE VIEW, YET, THE ABILITY TO SEE BEAUTY IN EVERY VIEW."
NATASHA ROCCA DEVINE

VALUE...

YOU.

YOUR **NATURAL TALENTS.**

YOUR **FAMILY.**

YOUR **FRIENDS.**

PEOPLE WHO HELP YOU IN EACH DAY.

ALWAYS VALUE YOUR **HEALTH** IN EACH DAY.

NEVER FORGET THEIR VALUE OR YOUR VALUE=**PRICELESS**

VULNERABILITY

ALLOW YOURSELF THE FREEDOM TO BE VULNERABLE.
BE YOURSELF IN EVERY MOMENT.
LET GO AND IF YOU FEEL VULNERABLE ACCEPT IT.
ACCEPT BEING YOURSELF IS YOUR BIGGEST STRENGTH.
VULNERABILTITY=BEING YOU IN NOW= BEING STRONG.

"Out of your vulnerabilities will come your strength." **Sigmund Freud**

WALK

WALK IT OUT. IF IT IS TO AND FROM WORK. WALKING TO THE SHOPS, THE PARK OR EVEN UP AND DOWN THE STAIRS… WALKING ALLOWS FOR SPONTANEITY AND IS GREAT FOR EXERCISE...

WAVELENGTH

PLEASE ONLY SURROUND YOURSELF WITH PEOPLE ON YOUR WAVELENGTH. Nrd

WISDOM

"Wisdom is the supreme part of happiness." Sophocles

"A warrior is about absolute vulnerability." *The Peaceful Warrior*

WORDS

WHAT YOU SPEAK IS INDICATIVE OF HOW YOU THINK OR FEEL AND ESSENTIALLY HOW YOU ACT IN EACH DAY…

TASK: NOTICE IF YOUR WORDS ARE CONSTANTLY NEGATIVE, WORK ON CHANGING THIS.

POSITIVE WORDS=POSITIVE THOUGHTS =POSITIVE ACTIONS.

TASK: START NOW AND YOU WILL SEE HOW ONE POSITIVE MOMENT CAN TURN INTO A POSITIVE DAY AND SO ON...NATASHA RD.

WORK

As the world is in a recession, there is a lot of stress and contention around 'who is to blame'? Everyone has his or her own opinions on this.

YET, IN LIFE, THERE IS ALWAYS SOMEONE TO BLAME FOR PROBLEMS THAT EFFECT YOUR LIFE. PLEASE REMEMBER ANGER HURTS ONLY YOU... WHY HURT YOURSELF FOR OTHERS?

SO, INSTEAD OF WASTING YOUR ENERGY BLAMING, WHY DON'T YOU CREATE A JOB AND SECURITY FOR YOU? YOUR FAMILY?

I come from an Irish-Italian family where a balance between a hard work ethic and committed family life is innate. Also, as my skills are creatively related with no direct route, it has always been up to myself to create my own work. Like with this book and in life, I now know that anything is possible if you are positive, focused and are not afraid of hard work...

Yet, no job is 'perfect' so each day should be focused on finding a balance. Yet, "The best way to appreciate your job is to imagine yourself without one." Oscar Wilde

TODAY TECHNOLOGY HAS CUT LIMITS IN WORK. NOW, IT IS YOU TO FIGHT YOUR FEARS AND TO LET GO OF YOUR LIMITS... FIND WORK=BALANCE!

NOW: CREATE A JOB THAT ALLOWS YOU TO USE YOUR NATURAL SKILLS IN EACH DAY
QUESTION TIME:
WHAT ARE MY NATURAL SKILLS?
WHAT JOB CAN I CREATE OR FIND TO USE THESE SKILLS?
START CREATING TODAY. IT IS UP TO YOU!

"FIND YOUR PASSION. CREATE WORK FROM HERE... YOU WILL SEE MAGIC COME TO LIFE." NRD

OF COURSE, everyone needs financial security of a job but nowadays there are so many options for this. You may be a full-time mother, run a company, or an artist, entrepreneur, athlete, or chef.

YET, EVERYONE DESERVES TO BE HAPPY IN HIS
OR HER WORK AND LIFE. YOU CAN AND SHOULD
FIND THE JOB OR INTEREST THAT IS BEST FOR
YOU… A JOB WHERE YOU CAN BE YOU. NRD.

"Everyone has been made for
some particular work, and the
desire for that work has been
put in every heart." Rumi

WORRY

WORRY WILL PARALYSE YOU FROM LIVING IN
THE MOMENT. PLEASE REMEMEMBER THAT THERE
ARE ALWAYS SOLUTIONS!

*TO DO: FIND AN ACTIVITY THAT WILL MOVE
YOU OUT OF WORRY AND BACK INTO ACTION.
BACK INTO THE MOMENT: A WALK, TALKING
WITH SOMEONE, WRITING IT DOWN, ANYTHING
OTHER THAN WORRY ITSELF.

REMEMBER, THIS TOO WILL PASS.
GET BACK INTO NOW… Nrd

"If this is redemption,
why do I bother at all,
There's nothing to mention,
and nothing has changed.
Still I'd rather be working at something,
than praying for the rain.
So I wander on,
till someone else is saved."
James Vincent McMorrow, Irish singer/songwriter.

WRITING

Writing for me has been a lifelong passion and something I practice naturally each day.

Writing is a way to record memories. More importantly, to create and capture new ideas. My studies in Journalism assisted me in harnessing my passion into a skill. Like pictures for a photographer, my words make up my images. I encourage others to follow this path of writing.

In everything I do, I embrace spontaneity as the creativity will not come through force. It may not be each morning but I recommend in writing down your ideas and thoughts at least once a week. To let go and clear space for new ideas… AND TO CREATE OPPORTUNITIES AND ENJOY EACH DAY.

TASK: BUY A NEW NOTEPAD. KEEP IT BESIDE YOUR BED, IN YOUR SPORTSBAG, OR ANYWHERE WHERE YOU CAN ACCESS IT EACH DAY OR WEEK. WHEN THOUGHTS, IDEAS OR PLANS COME INTO YOUR MIND (POSITIVE AND NEGATIVE) WRITE THEM DOWN.

*WRITING + THOUGHTS=
IDEAS=
THOUGHTS INTO ACTION=
CREATIVITY. Natasha RD

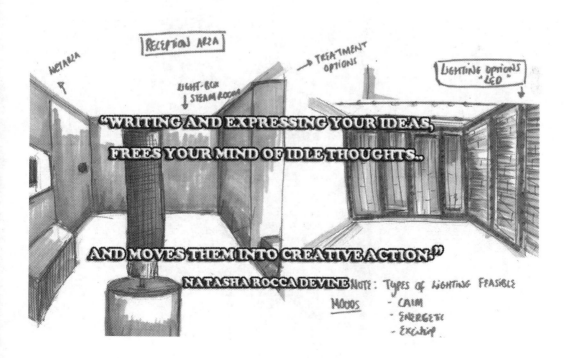

X-RAY STAR

According to Merriam-Webster dictionary, an X ray star is "a luminous celestial object emitting a major portion of its radiation in the form of X-rays —called also *X-ray source.*"

SO, BE AN X-RAY STAR. ALLOW YOURSELF TO SHINE…nrd.

"EVERYONE HAS THE X-FACTOR, IT IS UP TO YOU TO NOT ONLY FIND IT, BUT THEN ACCEPT IT AND ALLOW YOURSELF TO USE THIS EACH DAY...EMBRACE YOU." NRD

Yes

SAY YES TO OPPORTUNITIES IN LIFE. FIGHT YOUR FEARS... LIVE FOR NOW.

YOGA

After my accident, for exercise, I tried various methods of yoga such as Hatha Yoga and Bikram Yoga. At this time, I was still recovering and running and other impact sports were causing me migraines and pain. So, in my case, this helped me to detox and continue with my daily exercise.

Of course, each person has their own reason to practice yoga; tradition, meditation for the mind, to sculpt the body (to stretch or to build stamina) or all of the above. Now, there are so many types available, even hip-hop yoga! So, here are a few options to suit your needs.

Bikram Yoga
Bikram Yoga, founded by Bikram Choudry, is a series of 26 Hatha Yoga postures and two Pranayama breathing exercises that provide a challenging, invigorating, rejuvenating yoga experience. Done in a hot room for 90 minutes, this yoga works every muscle, tendon, ligament, joint and internal organ in the entire body.

Shadow Yoga
Shadow Yoga, founded by Zhander Remete, is Hatha Yoga integrating common principles of yoga asana, martial arts, dance and Ayurvedic/Siddha medicine. From a yogic perspective, "shadow" refers to our being's layers (5 koshas/sheaths) - physical, energetic, mental/emotional, wisdom and spirit bodies.

As an enlightened yogi once stated, "the appearance of this body is nothing but frozen layers of shadows."

Vinyasa Yoga

Vinyasa yoga is the unique style of Shiva Rea, a latest evolution of Prana Flow Yoga. It incorporates asana, creative flows, backbends, arm balances and integrated pranayama as a moving meditation while providing you tools to navigate with grace, power and confidence.

"Nothing can steal happiness, peace away from you: if anyone does make you angry, you are the loser: if someone can allow you to lose peace, you are the loser." Bikram Choudhury

"Yoga cannot cure every condition, but it can substantially help most of them." Richard Munro, Ph.D., of Cambridge, England

"Yoga is almost like music in a way: there's no end to it." Sting

"You cannot do yoga. Yoga is your natural state. What you can do are yoga exercises, which may reveal to you where you are resisting your natural state." Sharon Gannon

YOU

WHEN YOU ARE LIVING IN BALANCE AND IN THE MOMENT, YOU ARE THE BEST VERSION OF YOU. STOP TRYING TO BE 'THE BEST'. JUST BE YOU.

BEING YOU, YOU ARE ALREADY THE BEST WITHOUT TRYING.
(SIMPLE ☺). NATASHA RD

"Remind yourself, Nobody built like you, you design yourself." Jay Z- A Dream

Z_{EN}

"Zen is not some kind of excitement, but concentration on our usual everyday routine." Shunryu Suzuki

"Children are natural Zen masters: their world is brand new in each and every moment." John Bradshaw

ZEN=LIVING IN THE MOMENT. NRD

THE END...

BUT REALLY,
IT IS ONLY THE BEGINNING...

"VIVA PER ORA"

NATASHA ROCCA DEVINE: A.K.A.NRD.

REFERENCES:
BOOKS:

Boland, Margaret. Metamorphosis Seminar Notes.

Cameron, Julia. The Vein of Gold, A Journey to Your Creative Heart,
Pan Books, London, 1997

Jordan, Michael. I Can't Accept Not Trying: Michael Jordan on The Pursuit
of Excellence. Harper San Francisco, 1994

Jung, Carl. Man and his Symbols, Aldus Books Ltd, 1964

Lipton, Bruce H. and Bhaerman, Steve. Spontaneous Evolution: our
positive future (and a way to get there from here). Hay House, 2009

Oliver, Duncan. Coffee with the Buddha, Duncan Baird Publishers London,
2007

Schneider, Michael S. A Beginners Guide to constructing the universe - A
voyage from 1 to 10,

Tolle, Eckhart. The Power of Now, A guide to Spiritual Enlightenment,
Hodder & Stoughton, U.K., 1999.

SITES:

Acupressure:
www.acupressure.com

Acupuncture:
http://www.tcmci.ie/acupuncturefaqs.php

Alla Svirinskaya:
http://www.allasvirinskaya.com/

Aromatherapy:
www.naha.org
www.pacificinstituteofaromatherapy.com

Astrology:
http://www.astrologycom.com/index.html

Aura Soma:
http://www.indigochild.net/a_die_indigo_kinder_aura-soma.htm
www.thecolourrose.com
www.aura-soma.net

Bikram Yoga:
http://blog.gaiam.com/quotes/authors/bikram-choudhury

Chiropractic:
www.amerchiro.org
www.chiropractic.org
www.worldchiropracticalliance.org
www.10ac.com

Food:
http://www.cnngo.com/explorations/eat/readers-choice-worlds-50-
most-delicious-foods-012321
http://www.epicurious.com/articlesguides/blogs/80dishes

SITES:

Kinesiology:
www.icak.com
www.uskinesiologyinstitute.com

Metamorphosis-MARGARET BOLAND-Robert St John:
http://www.metamorphosis-rstjohn.com/

Music therapy:
www.musictherapy.org
www.soundlistening.com

Osteopathic Medicine:
www.cranialacademy.com
www.holisticmedicine.org

Reflexology:
www.reflexology-usa.org

Reiki:
http://www.reiki.ca/faqs.htm

Religions:
http://www.bbc.co.uk/religion/religions/
http://dictionary.reference.com/

N.R.D BIOGRAPHY:

Natasha Rocca Devine is a 27 Year old Irish-Italian Lighting Designer and Communications Specialist. She has both a Masters in Journalism and Media Communications and Interior Architecture. She has taken courses in Light engineering and design, Fashion design and through practice, taught herself Graphic Design. Natasha owned an online production company and wrote, produced and presented her own online documentaries. Meanwhile, she worked in front and behind camera for various small and large films, documentaries and online productions.

Each day, she practices Metamorphosis, designing and journaling her skills. Her passion for exercise is innate and remains a daily ritual. Natasha adores her family, friends, health, sport, music, travel, lighting, art, architecture and photography. She believes that living in the moment in balance, happiness and creativity is possible for all. Currently, she is living in Europe while visiting Boston, her American 'home from home'.